Building faith in the
Christadelphian community.

TIDINGS

Volume 86, Number 5 / May, 2023

IN THIS ISSUE

Editorial — Hezekiah's Path to Unity, **Dave Jennings** 2
Life Application — The Bully in the Pulpit and Pew, **Melinda Flatley**. 7
   — Coping with Bereavement, **Stephen Hill** 12
Prayer — Why Does God Encourage Us to Pray?, **Dev Ramcharan** 19
Exhortation and Consolation — Above and Beyond, **Peter Wilson**. 23
   — Paul's Road to Damascus Conversion, **Albert Cruz**. 31
Music and Praise — How Can I, Even I, Be Creative?, **Jessica Gelineau**. .34
Exposition — God is Not a Monster Part 4, **Chris Sales** 40
First Principles — The Righteous Shall Live By Faith, Part 3,
   Richard Morgan 45
Letters to the Editor 50
First Principles — Bethel, **Peter Hemingray** 58
Preaching and Teaching — A Taste of Guatemala, **Sam Robinson** 59
   — New Preaching Resource, **Art Courtenel** 61
Thoughts on the Way — Why Two Different Emblems?, **George Booker** . .62

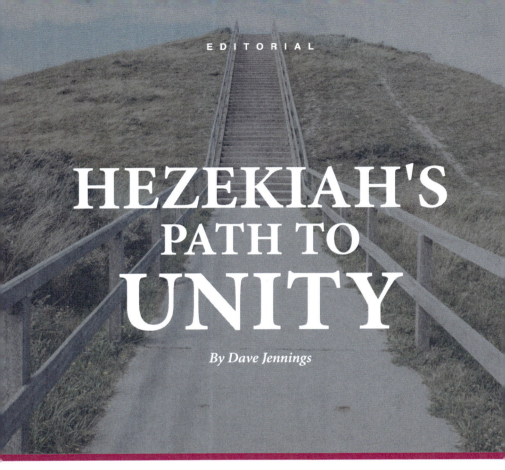

EDITORIAL

HEZEKIAH'S PATH TO UNITY

By Dave Jennings

FAITHFUL men and women have always turned to God's wisdom to identify and apply righteous principles to their steps. David concluded, *"Thy Word is a lamp unto my feet, and a light unto my path."* (Psa 119:105) When the way is unclear, and the pathway seems blocked, we must turn to Divine principles to move forward. When we see fragmentation and division of believers, what Godly principles may we find to heal the breach and glorify our Heavenly Father as one?

King Hezekiah began his reforms on the first month and the first day of the month of his reign. At just age twenty-five, he had a clear vision for the reform he wished to lead and proceeded with great urgency. In just sixteen days, he overturned the neglect and desecration of God's house done by his father, King Ahaz, which had occurred over sixteen years.

His initial focus was on the restoration of the Temple. His father had gathered and cut the vessels of the house in pieces, shut up the doors, built altars in every corner of Jerusalem, and encouraged burning incense to other Gods. (2 Chr 28:24-25). Besides cleaning up the filthiness from the holy place, Hezekiah was intensely concerned with the restoration of the people. First, the Levites needed to be reinstated, as they would be the ones to lead the worship. The work of the sanctification of the house came before the people themselves were sanctified.

But Hezekiah's reform was not only about the Temple, Jerusalem, or even Judah. He sought unity with all of Israel. He invited all tribes, from the south to the north, from *"Beersheba even to Dan,"* to join Judah in keeping the Passover. (2 Chr 30:5). It was a noble call to brethren long dispossessed in the north to join together in a unity of fellowship. He called them to abandon their old ways and historical failures and join with Judah as a righteous people in worship. To become a righteous people in worship, all had to go through a cleansing process. Hezekiah knew north and south tribes would be stronger people together than apart and that it would please the LORD.

Surely, Hezekiah must have known this would be a long shot at best. Most people in the north didn't want to keep the Passover, and many had long ago forgotten the Holy One of Israel. Yet, the appeal was broadly made, not only to those he anticipated would attend (Judah) but to all tribes.

Predictably, Hezekiah's appeal was not well received. This king, who was honestly pursuing righteousness, was laughed at, scorned, and mocked (30:10). To come to Judah to worship in Jerusalem was counter to their historical identity, dating back to the time of Jeroboam. But some heard the appeal and were moved to come to Jerusalem. *"Divers of Asher and Manasseh and of Zebulun humbled themselves, and came to Jerusalem."* (2 Chr 30:11). Verse 18 includes the tribe of Ephraim as one that joined them also.

The Scriptural record doesn't describe the disappointment Hezekiah felt from the mocking and scorning he received from the other tribes. The limited results couldn't have been what he had hoped for. But Hezekiah seems to accept those who were willing-hearted rather than obsessing over those who did not respond.

The keeping of Passover was held a month late on *"the fourteenth day of the second month."* (v. 15). This was permitted under the Law, allowing for those who were unclean because of touching a dead body, or were on a journey far off. (Num 9:10-11). This delay appears to have been done in this case because the priests were not yet sanctified, and they felt ashamed of not being ready. (2 Chr 30:15).

Still, many were not yet sanctified, especially the large mass of their northern brethren from Ephraim, Manasseh, Asher, and Zebulun. The temple was ready for Passover. The priests now were. Many of the people of Judah were. But these brethren who came desiring unity were not. What to do?

What Hezekiah did was pray.

The good LORD pardon every one that prepareth his heart to seek God, the LORD God of his fathers, though he be not cleansed according

> *Unity nurtures good works and removes harmful barriers, especially for our young people. It may even bring those who are detached from the community back to fellowship.*

to the purification of the sanctuary. (2 Chr 30:18-19).

The conditions of Hezekiah's wonderful appeal for unity were not perfect. A man of lesser faith might have delayed the celebration, or worse yet, go ahead without the LORD's blessing. This lesson is important to all seeking unity. Conditions will rarely be perfect. Timing may not be ideal. But the faithful take these inconsistencies and conundrums before God in prayer.

In one of the most beautiful verses in our Bible, the LORD *"hearkened"* to the prayer of Hezekiah, and He *"healed the people."* The Hebrew word for *"healed"* is *raphah*, which means to mend or stitch together. It is the same word used by Isaiah, where we are told *"the chastisement of our peace was upon him, and with his stripes we are* **healed**.*"* (Isa 53:5).

What a marvelous phrase! The LORD *"healed the people."* What was impossible under the Law, God did more than permit; he stitched these willing parties together. The Law would have technically prohibited their worship, but God looked into their willing hearts and saw the promise of unity between brethren.

The excitement of unity was so profound that the people invoked a practice from the time of Solomon (1 Kgs 8:65), extending the Passover celebration for an additional week. Beyond this, we are told that even more, this unity attracted the *"strangers that came out of the land of Israel, and dwelt in Judah."* (2 Chr 30:25).

When unity occurs, excitement permeates all aspects of spiritual life. It creates trust and confidence between brothers and sisters. It nurtures good works and removes harmful barriers, especially for our young people. It may even bring those who are detached from the community back to fellowship.

After this memorable Passover celebration, there was a commitment to destroy the images, groves, and high places in the land. In *"all Judah and Benjamin, in Ephraim also and Manasseh, they utterly destroyed them all."* (2 Chr 31:1). Later in Josiah's reign, the cleansing of images, groves, and high places continued in Manasseh, Ephraim, Simeon, and Naphtali. (2 Chr 34:6). It's clear the initial work for unity was very successful, but it required ongoing due diligence in the years to come to keep the people holy and separate from false gods.

The very connective tissue of unity is God healing us, stitching us together.

Editorial / Hezekiah's Path to Unity

When He does this, the conditions need not be perfect, but hearts need to be true. We, too, need to be "menders." Paul wrote in Galatians,

> Brethren, if a man be overtaken in a fault, ye which are spiritual, restore such an one in the spirit of meekness; considering thyself, lest thou also be tempted. (Gal 6:1).

The word *"restore"* is instructive. It is the word *katartizo*, which means to mend or repair. The same Greek word describes how the disciples were *"mending"* their nets by the seaside. (Matt 4:21). The word *katartizo* is used in Greek medical literature to set a bone. It is done gently and carefully, with longsuffering and patience to repair rather than discard.

As we look at unity in these Last Days, let's remember the important counsel from the time of Hezekiah.

1. Include unity in your personal vision of work in the truth.
2. Put aside historical disconnections and seek to heal breaches that may have existed for decades.
3. Lay the groundwork for unity by sanctifying yourself and being a dedicated, prayerful ecclesia; remember that all of us are only righteous through the grace of the Lord Jesus Christ.
4. Invite all without concern over how the appeal will be received. Accept those who respond as being who the LORD has provided. Work with them. No matter how small the size.
5. Make prayer a leading part of unity work. Pray God will heal us all, stitching together what we cannot. Rely on His wisdom, not our own.
6. Celebrate unity when it occurs. It is well worth taking the extra week as they did in Hezekiah's time!
7. Communicate broadly when unity is achieved, through God's grace. It may attract some who might otherwise have had no interest. Unity attracts people to God!

There are moments when I would love to have seen the majesty of the Scriptures unfold. To marvel at the beauty of the Garden. To see the great

---

The word "restore" is instructive. It is the word katartizo, which means to mend or repair. The same Greek word describes how the disciples were "mending" their nets by the seaside.

deliverance of Israel at the Red Sea. To sit at the feet of our Lord during his sermons. I would have loved to have been in Jerusalem when it was said,

> Then the priests the Levites arose and blessed the people: and their voice was heard, and their prayer came up to his holy dwelling place, even unto heaven." (2 Chr 30:27).

Unity wasn't possible for the tribes who had laughed and scorned Hezekiah's appeal. Unity wasn't possible for those who rejected the God of Israel. But for those seeking Him, those doing so with pure and contrite hearts, they received a blessing that would shape their lives.

The unity King Hezekiah appealed for over 2,500 years ago was later made possible by his greater son, the Lord Jesus Christ. The Lord petitioned his Father for the unity of believers through the truth. His prayer was that we might *"be one, as thou, Father, art in me, and I in thee, that they also may be one in us: that the world may believe that thou hast sent me."* (John 17:21). Will we humble ourselves to respond to his appeal?

As David wrote,

> Behold, how good and how pleasant it is for brethren to dwell together in unity! It is like the precious ointment upon the head, that ran down upon the beard, even Aaron's beard: that went down to the skirts of his garments; As the dew of Hermon, and as the dew that descended upon the mountains of Zion: for there the LORD commanded the blessing, even life for evermore. (Psa 133).

It may be that the optimum conditions for achieving unity is when brothers and sisters thirst for it, when they see it as *"precious ointment"* or the *"dew of Hermon."* But it begins with someone reaching out, as King Hezekiah did. May we all put unity on our personal and ecclesial agenda. Fellowship is not of human origin. God designed, introduced, and made it possible through our Lord. Any unity must start from Aaron's head and work its way down the beard. From top to bottom. Let's trust that He is the one who has the answers. May God heal us all.

Dave Jennings

THE BULLY IN THE PULPIT AND THE PEW

By Melinda Flatley

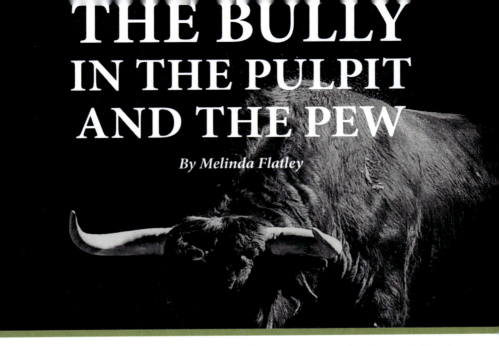

WHEN we envision bullying, we commonly think it's a problem mostly happening in schools. And lately, it has taken on the dimensions of an epidemic. According to current statistics, 20 % of young people aged 12 to 18 reported being bullied.[1] Schools are supposed to be places of refuge. And so are churches.

Bullying is a widespread act that spans all ages, genders, and localities. There is a growing trend of adult-on-adult bullying in churches and adult venues. A recent survey estimates 30% of adults have experienced bullying in these places.[2] You might be thinking, "Not in my ecclesia. No way." If only it were that easy to reject the idea outright! It is sad to think adults can display bullying behavior just the same as kids. One would hope all school bullies have grown up and stopped the unacceptable behaviors of their youth. Unfortunately, it is not always the case, even in ecclesias, Bible School and reunion committees, AB meetings, or church social events.

What is it?

Let's take a look at how bullying is defined so we can gain insight into if we experience the behavior in our church.

"Bullying is an ongoing and deliberate misuse of power in relationships through repeated verbal, physical and/or social behaviour (sic) that intends to cause physical, social and/or psychological harm. It can involve an individual or a group misusing their power, or perceived power, over one or more persons who feel unable to stop it from happening."[3]

Bullying takes many forms. It is bullying in your ecclesia if you:

- Form a clique and exclude others who are less popular.
- Pass on negative gossip and rumors about a church member.
- Make fun of a fellow Christadelphian.
- Insist your interpretation of a Bible passage is the only way.
- Create new First Principles the ecclesia must observe.
- Challenge those whose lifestyle you disagree with, such as hobbies, outside friends, marriage partners, or holidays celebrated.
- Prevent others, such as sisters or young people, from using their talents in ecclesial work.
- Block others from suggesting changes because "We need to adhere to our traditions."
- Criticize a brother or sister's apparel, weight, hairstyle or other physical attributes.
- Comment disparagingly on another family's parenting style.
- Compare yourself favorably to others' attendance records at ecclesial events.
- Consider yourself the one who keeps the Truth pure by dictating practices and beliefs.
- Claim to be God's spokesperson. "God says..."
- Become involved in sexual abuse.
- Act on jealous feelings about other church members' accomplishments.
- Stand by and do not intervene when you observe bullying.
- Withhold forgiveness and fellowship to repentant sinners.

While adult church bullies rarely use physical confrontation (although I once observed a fistfight having to be broken up in the ecclesial lobby), verbal assaults, even when subtle, can be quite damaging.[3] Another method is using "keyboard courage" to post derogatory,

While the word bullying doesn't show up, we do find men described as "brutish."...The Hebrew connotes "stupid, foolish and irrational as cattle." Brutish people, or bullies, then are seen as acting like beasts.

Life Application / The Bully in the Pulpit and the Pew

dishonest, deprecating language and unflattering photos about their targets on social media.

What Does the Bible Say about Bullying?

Quite a bit, actually. While the word bullying doesn't show up, we do find men described as *"brutish." "For he seeth that wise men die, likewise the fool and the brutish person perish, and leave their wealth to others."* (Psa 49:10 KJV).[4] The Hebrew connotes "stupid, foolish and irrational as cattle." Brutish people, or bullies, then are seen as acting like beasts.

Proverbs 6:16-19 tells us the behaviors God abhors:

> *There are six things that the LORD hates, Seven that are an abomination to Him: Haughty eyes, a lying tongue, And hands that shed innocent blood, A heart that devises wicked plans, Feet that run rapidly to evil, A false witness who declares lies, And one who spreads strife among brothers.*

The first bully in the Scriptures was Cain. He was jealous of his brother Abel's successful sacrifice, so he accosted and killed him. Further in the line of Cain, we read about Lamech, who *"killed a man for wounding me."* (Gen 4:23). We learn of Pharaoh's bullying of the children of Israel and Moses, their redeemer. His brothers hated Joseph because of the coat of many colors and his righteousness. Before David became king, Saul bullied him, seeking to kill him numerous times. Later, David exercised his power over Bathsheba and Uriah to ravish and murder. King Ahab and Queen Jezebel used their positions to destroy Naboth and his family to obtain his garden. The satraps plotted to get rid of Daniel by tricking King Darius into making a declaration about god worship by the irrevocable Law of the Medes and Persians. The story of Esther and Mordecai relates how Haman persecuted them. King Zedekiah cast Jeremiah in a mud pit to bury the uncomfortable truth of his prophecy. Herod Antipas imprisoned John the Baptist for rebuking him and Herodias about their illicit marriage. Then Herod was tricked by Herodias and her daughter, Salome, to have John beheaded. The Apostle Paul was opposed by many, including the Jewish party of the circumcision, the Romans, and two metal workers, Demetrius, the silversmith, and Alexander, the coppersmith. The owners of a nameless slave girl in Philippi took advantage of her frail mental state to gain wealth. There are many more we could identify. As you do your readings, see if you can pick up on this theme.

We cannot, however, omit talking about the most bullied person in the Bible: our Lord Jesus Christ. His enemies, the Scribes and Pharisees, followed him about attempting to get him to say or do something they could charge him with. He was the subject of evil rumors. They finally arrested, tortured, tried and crucified him, all because they were jealous of his power. Nevertheless, even though they exercised their own immediate power over Christ, it did not last long. Three days later, the Lord was resurrected and now sits at God's right hand, disseminating God's will in the nations.

Looking at this example of Jesus, who was sinless, those who are targets of a bully should know it is not so much about them but the aggressor. Being bullied is NOT a sign of personal weakness. Sometimes subjects of bullying are advised to strike back—that's how it works in the schoolyard. But, in our ecclesias, there are better strategies, such as confiding in a trusted brother or sister who can advocate for them.

So, What Can We Do?

We need first to be aware that bullying does occur in our ecclesias. Paul reminds us of what our attitude should

So, as those who have been chosen of God, holy and beloved, put on a heart of compassion, kindness, humility, gentleness, and patience; bearing with one another, and forgiving each other, whoever has a complaint against anyone; just as the Lord forgave you, so must you do also. In addition to all these things put on love, which is the perfect bond of unity. (Col 3:12-14).

To whom is this advice given? Answer: to all of us! Jesus taught: *"Do not judge according to appearance, but judge with righteous judgment."* (John 7:24). Furthermore, he says,

A new commandment I give to you, that you love one another, even as I have loved you, that you also love one another. (John 13:34 KJV).

Rather than dismissing the subject of church bullies as absurd and nonexistent, let's acknowledge it exists. Let's take the time to observe ecclesial interactions.

For the whole Law is fulfilled in one Word, in the statement, "YOU SHALL LOVE YOUR NEIGHBOR AS YOURSELF." But if you bite and devour one another, take care that you are not consumed by one another. (Gal 5:14-15).

Acting in love is the exact opposite of biting and devouring. Unless we have been subjected to harassment ourselves, it may be hard for us to know what to do about it. We may not realize the depth of the pain caused. The consequences for both the victim and the perpetrator can be grave. Depression, loneliness, lack of trust, illness, fear, low self-esteem, school and work problems, and thoughts of "bullycide" often follow victims for years. The situation can become the reason someone leaves the Truth. That's why it's imperative to recognize unhealthy situations and help both sides of the bullying equation. It requires proactive measures to stand up and get them help. There's a saying: It takes two to create abuse: the bully and the bystander who does not intervene.

Rather than dismissing the subject of church bullies as absurd and nonexistent, let's acknowledge it exists. Let's take the time to observe ecclesial interactions. Even before you need them, brainstorm strategies to help prevent and assist the bullied and the bully. And, above all, ask as David did:

Investigate my life, O God, find out everything about me; Cross-examine and test me, Get a clear picture of what I'm about; See for yourself whether I've done anything wrong—then guide me on the road to eternal life. (Psa 139:23-24 MSG).

*Melinda Flatley,
Pittsburgh Ecclesia, PA*

---

[1] National Bullying Prevention Center. https://www.pacer.org/bullying/info/stats.asp.
[2] Doctors of Osteopathic Medicine. https://findado.osteopathic.org/adult-bullying-survey-finds-31-americans-bullied-adult.
[3] National Center Against Bullying. ncab.org.au/bullying-advice/bullying-for-parents/definition-of-bullying/.
[4] All Scriptural citations are taken from the New American Standard Bible unless otherwise noted.

COPING WITH BEREAVEMENT

By Stephen Hill

WHY am I writing about grief? It is seldom discussed or written about because it is not a positive or uplifting subject. The loss of loved ones in my life, especially my daughter's death, has caused me to think deeply about grief and what the Bible says about this emotional and very personal subject. I would like to share my thoughts and experiences in two articles.

Our eldest daughter Alison was born in Toronto, Canada. We returned to Australia, where she grew up, accepted Christ in baptism, and married a brother in Christ. At age twenty-two, she died in a road accident. Now, twenty-nine years later, the impact of our loss is still keenly felt. Over the following two years, I endeavored to understand God's perspective on such a tragedy. To my surprise,, there is much information on grief in the Bible. This awareness reinforced my appreciation of this amazing book–a book that fulfills every need we can have in life. Truly God has provided "all things that pertain to life and godliness." (2 Pet 1:3).[1]

The Reality of Death

The subject of death and the consequent grief should not be strange for us. The mortality of man is one of our first principles; indeed, I would argue it is **the** first principle. From it comes our need for salvation from death, the means of salvation in Christ and fulfillment of that process in God's Kingdom on earth.

The foundation of God's revelation is in Genesis:

> "Genesis is the seed-plot of the whole Bible. It is essential to the true understanding of its every part. It is the foundation on which Divine Revelation rests; and on which it is built. It is not only the foundation of all Truth, but it enters into, and forms part of all subsequent inspiration; and is at once the warp and woof of Holy Writ. Genesis is quoted or referred to sixty times in the New Testament; and divine authority is set like a seal on its historical facts." (Bullinger).[2]

In Genesis we learn that:

- We all return to the ground at death (3:19).
- There may be a premature, or violent death (4:8).
- Every generation dies—*"and he died"* (5:5).

Furthermore, we read that disease, famine, and war all reap their harvest. Trouble is inevitable:

- *"Man is born to trouble as the sparks fly upward."* (Job 5:7).
- *"In the world you will have tribulation."* (John 16:33).
- *"We were troubled on every side… inside were fears."* (2 Cor 7:4-5).
- *"The fiery trial which is to try you."* (1 Pet 4:12-13).

What is Grief?

Grief is the physical and emotional response to the loss of something or someone we love. Similar experiences can occur with unemployment, serious illness, personal offense, a loved one hurting, marriage failure, the death of a loved one, a miscarriage, an ecclesial dispute, or a rebellious child. Grief can be particularly deep when it is unexpected.

Unfortunately, when it comes to our personal experiences, there is little spoken or written about in our community. Historically there was a sense of "toughing it out" or "having a stiff upper lip." This attitude has made it more difficult to cope, both for the bereaved and the mourners.

Given the breadth and depth of information we have in the Bible, our expectations of life should be realistic. So much of the Bible deals with real people in real-life experiences. It is not just a book of doctrines. How thankful we should be that it is so! Therefore, we discover that many others have had the same or similar experiences in every generation–we are not alone.

Death brings sorrow and pain:
- "She laid her hand on her head and went away crying bitterly." (2 Sam 13:19).
- "Alas! Alas!" (1 Kgs 13:30; Jer 22:18; Amos 5:16).
- "I bowed down heavily." (Psa 35:14).
- "I mourned like a dove." (Isa 38:14; 59:11).
- "I will wail and howl" (Mic 1:8).
- "As one grieves for a firstborn." (Zech 12:10).
- "A sword will pierce through your own soul." (Luke 2:35).

Loss and grief are the prices we pay for living and loving. We would not feel grief if we didn't love anything or anyone. Bereavement brings a new awareness of the fragility of life.

It is important to appreciate that grief has two parts:
1. The loss of part of oneself, something of great value.
2. We also grieve for unfulfilled dreams and for the future that will never be.

Either of these can be dominant depending on our circumstances.

Normal Grief Reactions

One's response to loss comes in various forms. While there are many common reactions, each individual's grief is unique. The reason is because we are all different in temperament, and our relationships with loved ones are unique. Nevertheless, the following physical and emotional reactions are common:

Physical:
- Tightness in the throat, difficulty swallowing.
- Choking, shortness of breath.
- Sighing respiration.
- An empty feeling in the abdomen.
- Altered sleep patterns.
- Loss of appetite.
- Restless activity–disorganized, aimless behavior.
- Inability to concentrate or make plans or decisions.
- Weeping, often without prompting.

> *Given the breadth and depth of information we have in the Bible, our expectations of life should be realistic.*

Life Application / Coping With Bereavement

> *Not only are our responses to loss variable, but they change over time.*

Emotional:

- Depression.
- Emotional pain.
- Rapid changes in feelings from love to grief to anger to guilt.
- The thought that things are unreal, a sense of unreality, that one will wake up and find it is just a bad dream.
- Feelings of regret, yearning, and longing to put things right. "I should have." "I should not have."
- Exaggerated blame of self.
- A certainty that we have seen or heard the deceased for a fleeting second.
- Preoccupation with the deceased and parallel withdrawal from activities.
- Dread that one is losing faith or going crazy.
- Nothing seems pleasurable or meaningful. "What is the use?"

Knowing that what we are going through is not unusual is helpful. Much will depend on our circumstances and how we deal with these responses. There is an element of unavoidability, but we can also act to modify our responses, particularly as time progresses.

Dealing with Death

What do I do now that it has happened? What am I going to do about it? I have found the story of Job very helpful. This is something that may seem strange, as I have encountered many brothers and sisters who find this book confusing or depressing. Let's consider a few points that comfort me:

- All of Job's children died–all ten! (1:2, 19). I have only lost one of my three children.
- *"The Lord gave and the Lord has taken away"* (1:21). Our children are a gift from God and are returned to Him when they are baptized.
- Job's wife (equally, if not more so, affected) reacted differently to him (2:9). My wife Dianne and I did not react the same way to the death of our daughter. Neither was our subsequent journey through grief exactly the same.
- His three friends came to visit, and they said nothing (very wise of them–what do you say anyway?) (2:11, 13). They **did** visit, even though they would not have enjoyed the experience.
- His grief was very great (2:13).
- But his losses were too great for him to bear, and he broke (wouldn't

you?) (3:1-26). This reaction was not prompted by any unhelpful comments by his friends.
- Job asked "Why?'" (3:11, etc.). God did respond, but not in the way he wanted or expected (38:1; 40:1). Job acknowledged that his challenge to God was wrong (42:5-6).

The Death of a Child

I think it is indisputable that the death of a child is the worst thing that can happen to a parent. It is their worst nightmare. This is because it is against the natural order. We all expect parents to die first and realize our marriage partner may die before us, but we never think about our child dying before us.

My daughter's death felt like, and still feels like losing a limb. The wound heals, but the limb does not regrow—the loss is permanent in this life. Even God, our Father, felt the death of His Son and covered the earth with darkness. The scene was too shocking to look upon (Luke 23:44-45).

Nevertheless, most, if not all, parents would say that if they had known they would only have their child for a few years, they would still have had them. Our love for another does not depend on them or how long we have known them. Like, God, we choose to love—unconditionally. Our God and His Son are the supreme examples of love. Their love for each of us is demonstrated over and over in Scripture. Examples of their love in the past show us how they still love us.

A brother wrote to us after Alison died: "One thing we know and are assured of is that the loss you suffer is felt by our heavenly Father, for Alison was His daughter also. Likewise, our Lord Jesus Christ who had compassion on those he healed in the days of his pilgrimage, will have the same compassion towards his brethren and sisters now."

What You Can Do to Help the Bereaved

There is much we can do to help the bereaved:

- Be warm and friendly in the good times so your help will be more readily received in bad times.
- Visit the bereaved (Job 2:11; John 11:19). Our **presence** says more than words.
- Reach out, often and repeatedly, to the person experiencing grief.
- Avoid evading the bereaved.
- Don't be put off if you are not wanted. Try again later (however, they may have enough help already, or even too much).
- You will not feel good about going but choose to go.
- The bereaved need company. They gain comfort from your presence, your acceptance of them, your consolation. They need warm affection and encouragement.
- Demonstrate that you **do** want to share their burden.
- Do not be ashamed of tears; they are a healthy release of emotion.
- *"Weep with those who weep."* (Rom. 12:15).
- Be patient and understanding, do not judge.
- You can't make them feel better; there is no comfort.
- Send messages (2 Sam 10:1-2) cards

Life Application / Coping With Bereavement

and letters. Write of your love and respect, of your memories of the one who has died, by name.

- Telephone, text, or write at **later** times, especially on the anniversary of the death. When it appears that everyone else has forgotten (they haven't), it is comforting to know others are thinking of you.
- Give food. They are not able to think about cooking and shopping at this time.
- Bring flowers to brighten and beautify.
- Go for walks with the bereaved.

But what do you say?

- You don't need to say anything special.
- Say "I care" and "God cares."
- Say what the dead person meant to **you**, mention their **name**, and reminisce (this gives the bereaved "permission" to talk if they want to).
- Encourage the bereaved to talk; it helps them to clarify their feelings, release their emotions, and receive reassurance.
- "What help can I be?"
- "How **are** you doing?" Show you mean it.

The bereaved need company. They gain comfort from your presence, your acceptance of them, your consolation. They need warm affection and encouragement.

- Do not ask them how they are unless you are prepared to hear the answer.
- Be prepared to hear about their unbearable pain.

Do not use clichés such as:

- "He had a good life" or "He is out of pain." These may be true but don't address their needs now.
- "She would not want you to grieve." How do you know, and what does this mean anyway? Their grief is because they loved so much.
- "You must keep up for the children's sake."
- "You are young; you will find another partner if you pray about it." This was actually said to our son-in-law!
- Don't say, "I know how you feel." You **do not** know how they feel.

Talking about the resurrection is fine, but that was probably never in doubt. Knowing there is a resurrection does **not** stop the grieving process (John 11:21-27, 32-33). It is not the future that is causing grief, but the present.

Listen. Learn how to be a good listener (Prov 18:13; Jas 1:19). "To listen well is as powerful a means of communication and influence as to talk well." (John Marshall).

Above all, pray. Pray for them and tell them you have. Do not feel this is strange or boastful. But we have found it immensely helpful. Consider how many times in the New Testament, prayer for others is mentioned. See the list in the endnotes.[3]

The case of Epaphras (Col 4:12) is very instructive. He was known for *"always labouring fervently for you in prayers."* Either Paul overheard his audible prayers, or they discussed their prayers with each other. Either way, this knowledge would have greatly encouraged the Colossians.

Stephen Hill,
Hyde Park Ecclesia, SA

Alison Downing, a sister in the Lord, aged 22

---

[1] All Scriptural citations are taken from the New King James Version, unless otherwise noted.
[2] Bullinger, E.W. *The Companion Bible of 1909–* Appendix 2. Grand Rapids: Kregel Publications, 1994.
[3] John 17:20; Luke 22:32; Rom 1:7-10; 15:5-6, 13, 33; 16:20, 25-27; 1 Cor 16:23; 2 Cor 1:2-4; 13:7, 14; Gal 6:16, 18; Eph 1:2, 15-23; 3:14-21; Phil 1:2-3, 9-11; 4:23; Col 1:2-3, 9-12; 2:1; 4:12, 18; 1 Thess 1:1-3; 3:11-13; 5:23-24, 28; 2 Thess 1:2, 11-12; 2:16; 3:16; 1 Tim 1:2; 6:21; 2 Tim 1:2-3, 16-18; 4:22; Titus 1:4; 3:15; Phm :3-6, 25; Heb 13:20-21, 25).

SPECIAL SECTION: PRAYER

WHY DOES GOD ENCOURAGE US TO

?

By Dev Ramcharan

Rejoice always, pray without ceasing, give thanks in all circumstances, for this is the will of God in Christ Jesus for you. (1 Thess 5:16-18 ESV).

WITHOUT a doubt, our relationship with God is the most important one in our lives. And yet, we all know that it waxes and wanes, affected by the vicissitudes of circumstance, health, and mood. That tendency toward inconstancy is not in Him; it is only in us. Sometimes we use Him like an ATM machine, drawing on Him only in times of need when crises consume us. But God is not a machine that satisfies our periodic or immediate needs. God is alive and feeling, and He expects us to invest all of who we are in our relationship with Him. We realize we often neglect this greatest of relationships, failing to devote the time we need to keep it healthy, growing, and deepening in love and understanding. As I reflect on my own relationship with the Father, who has saved me from hopelessness, it occurs to me that the quality of my prayers reflects the tone and depth of all of my relationships. There is much work to do.

We all know that comfortable rut we fall into, the repetitive conversations that keep us engaged in a kind of warm and safe dialogue free of the dangerous turbulence of utterly open and transparent conversation. God speaks to us frankly in His Word, sharing Himself, His hopes for His people, His pleas for their obedience and loyalty, His hurt when they reject Him, His deepest intentions and plans, and His desire to save us from sin and death. And most importantly, He tells us about a vast and deep love that moved Him to sacrifice His beloved son so we might have hope. God has invested so much in His relationship with us. His Word provides one half of a conversation, and we supply the other half through prayer. If my daily conversations with God are perfunctory, repetitive, superficial, and spoken or thought in a way that keeps Him at a "safe" distance from my wounds and my brokenness, then do I really love Him with all my heart, soul, and mind (Matt 22:37)? Do I trust Him (Prov 3:5-6)?

God encourages us through Paul to *"Rejoice always, pray without ceasing, give thanks in all circumstances; for this is the will of God in Christ Jesus for you."* (1 Thess 5:16-18). To paraphrase: "Talk to me; talk to me a lot, not only when things are good or when you're in terror and can't find a way out of trouble. I want you to share with me all the time." That is what the passage is saying to us. He wants to know us, and He wants us to know Him and to see ourselves more clearly. We all have an abiding need for connection. God made us connect to Him and each other. Often, we wish those closest to us knew us better and that we knew them better too. But vulnerability is hard in this superficial world of Facebook fake glamor and idealized self-promotion. Conversations that require the most vulnerable transparency between two people can alter the direction of a relationship and a life with a fiery, transformative power. But fire scorches, and these conversations involve courage and honest frankness that our culture avoids. If one starts with a decision to disclose, there is always the risk of rejection, scorn or mockery. Will this person I care about or love continue to love me if they see and hear all my towering babel of inconsistencies, weaknesses, frailties, and heart-rending sorrows? Will they still stand by me? Will they want me?

Job pours himself out to his friends, crying out with shocking public grief and disappointment, mingled with

> *As he speaks, we know we are pigmies beside him, for this is a godly and righteous giant of a man. He does not trundle out trite and well-worn phrases of the variety we can relate to in our public and private prayers.*

stubbornly held strands of hope that keep him tethered to an Almighty God he cannot understand. The person he has known and believed in all his life looks like He has abandoned him, and Job risks slipping into the encroaching darkness of despair as he contemplates the losses he has sustained and the grief that is drowning him. Uncomprehending friends exacerbate this grief with genuine initial efforts but then descend into the bitterest acrimony and condemnation. Job's anguished vulnerability and naked disclosure of what is in his heart surely move us to the core. Prayer is not poetry; it is not always pretty. Sometimes prayer is ugly, awkward, halting, and sometimes jumbled and inarticulate, but God considers our situation and condition and gives us compassionate help in that process (Rom 8:26-28).

Job's passionate and exhausted outpourings (his prayers) are dangerous conversations that culminate in God speaking out of a tempest that directly reflects the surging emotional waters in Job's heart. As he speaks, we know we are pigmies beside him, for this is a godly and righteous giant of a man. He does not trundle out trite and well-worn phrases of the variety we can relate to in our public and private prayers. He cries out in agony; he shrieks; he argues; he pleads; he is truly, wholly, and only himself without masks, shorn of subterfuge and any kind of pretense, utterly vulnerable and diseased, a brave and broken man. He, as good as accuses the LORD of not knowing what He is doing in bringing such horror into his life unjustly (in his mind). God does not strike him dead for impertinence. He knows the pain and turmoil this man is in. He stretches him to the breaking point and brings him closer to Him. Job's prayers are vivid and intense. God encourages us to cry out to Him, to connect with Him in honest and heartfelt prayer (Psa 34:6; 61:2; Lam 2:18).

In the end, Job does not get answers to his questions. He humbles himself before God, accepts His actions, and recognizes the enormity of his ignorance. God is not always easily understood, but His actions are to be accepted with humility and, in the end, in quietness. In compassion and with loving pity, God nurtures Job back to an even greater stage of maturity and strength. And what does God say to his friends? *"My servant Job shall **pray for you**, for I will **accept his prayer** not to deal with you according to your* *folly."* (Job 42:8-9). Job is transformed through the experience of bereavement, loss, prayer and contemplation of the words and works of El Shaddai. We sit in shocked wonder as we read this book and realize that God talks to each of us in our own storms. Sometimes it takes a storm to turn and burnish a human heart. It may take a wilderness wandering to change us. It may require a shuddering, sweaty, bloody night-time garden wailing to the Father, without eloquence, polish, or refinement of expression, to put us into His hands, to trust Him completely. And this kind of prayer makes us better people than the people around us.

Job prayed for his friends, and a key part of our prayer life must be a concern for and lifting up of prayer for others. Continuously doing this deepens our relationships with those we pray for and strengthens families and ecclesias. (Eph 6:18).

We are encouraged to pray for guidance. None of this life in the Truth is natural or easy for us. We stray so easily and often off the path we should be on. Thus, the Psalmist writes, *"Show me the right path, O LORD; point out the road for me to follow."* (Psa 25:4, NLT). Our only hope for remaining in the faith and healthy in it is through the work of God in our lives, so we need to constantly pray for Him to guide us. We bring our wounds and shame to the Father and continually pray for the forgiveness of our sin, an enduring need in the days of our flesh (Psa 51, 32).

We pray for God's Kingdom, *"Let your kingdom come!"* (Matt. 6:9-13) to keep that hope alive in our hearts. We pray for the preaching and the preachers of God's Truth so the Gospel message may be heard among us and in the world in this age suffused with darkness.

Paul writes to the Ephesians:

In all circumstances, take up the shield of faith, with which you can extinguish all the flaming darts of the evil one; and take the helmet of salvation, and the sword of the spirit, which is the Word of God, praying at all times in the spirit, with all prayer and supplication for all the saints, and also for me, that Words may be given to me in opening my mouth boldly to proclaim the mystery of the gospel… that I may declare it boldly, as I ought to speak. (Eph 6:16-20).

God encourages us to make prayer a living, daily, continuous conversation with Him. That conversation is greater than any other we could ever have, and it changes us, readying us for life to come. As in all things, we become better at it with practice, and in time we find ourselves praying all through the day. And in times of trouble, through prayer, we come to grips with situations and recognize who we are and who God is. In Job and our lives, we see that prayer is the anvil on which God hammers out an enlarged faith in his struggling children.

May we all become men and women of prayer, and may that have a transformative power for our community.

*Dev Ramcharan,
Toronto West Ecclesia, ON*

EXHORTATION AND CONSOLATION

ABOVE AND BEYOND

By Peter Wilson

THERE is a field in Southwest Arkansas called "Crater of the Diamonds State Park." For a small fee, people wander around in the field or scratch the surface, looking for diamonds. Some six hundred have been found this year, including a 2.8-carat one recently. The diamonds are usually just sitting on the surface or near the surface. They don't look like our concept of sparkling diamonds. They look like pebbles because they are uncut and unpolished. No heavy equipment is allowed. But if equipment were allowed, you can imagine the increased yield with a more intense approach to the search.

This story is a parable. Sometimes we, by choice, only just scratch the surface in Bible study. Even then, we still find some gems. We can do the readings faithfully but never ask questions. Questions like, "What is the lesson for me?" We can go decades reading a difficult portion of Scripture and never pursue such questions. We can passively sit in classes and never engage in ideas that are brought up to make them our own.

Today, our Scriptural field to explore is Psalms 119:97-104.

O how love I thy law! it is my meditation all the day. Thou through thy commandments hast made me wiser than mine enemies: for they are ever with me. I have more understanding than all my teachers: for thy testimonies are my meditation. I understand more than the ancients, because I keep thy precepts. I have refrained my feet from every evil way, that I might keep thy Word. I have not departed from thy judgments: for thou hast taught me. How sweet are thy Words unto my taste! yea, sweeter than honey to my mouth! Through thy precepts I get understanding: therefore I hate every false way.

The Organization

First, there is the Psalm's organization. Everything we learn about the organization helps us strengthen our understanding of its meaning. The structure helps us remember it, zero in on its key points, and ponder them.

It begins with a topic sentence in verse 97. This is what the section is about.

> "O how love I thy law! It is my meditation all the day."

It then moves to the body of the message in verses 98-102, which supports the idea of the topic sentence.

And finally, to the refrain in verses 103-104. This conclusion summarizes the preceding ideas in a slightly expanded form (connected to the key idea but not identical Wording). It also serves as a divider between this section and the next.

Recognizing this organizational outline helps us understand and remember the lessons of this particular psalm for us.

The Overall Structure

Then, there is the structure borrowed from the other twenty-one sections of Psalm 119. Every verse has one of nine synonyms for God's Word in it. This lets us know the overall theme of the entire Psalm 119 is the Word of God.

This Psalm introduces us to the Law, testimonies, commandments, precepts (twice), the Word (twice), and judgments. Everything else said in this section weaves its way around supporting this critical backbone.

This psalm section is poetry. It's unlike rhyming metric English poetry. Hebrew poetry depends on couplets (two connected sentences), which is no exception. A statement is given first, and then the second half of the couplet restates and expands the key idea: sometimes as cause and effect, sometimes as a building thought, and other times as a supporting double negative. Sometimes it's a triplet.

Music is powerful. It may be the only way to reach the depths of our emotions. It also helps us remember the words.

Here is what is important for us unpoetic Goyim to know. It's as if there is a tacit "and furthermore" between the two halves of the poetic couplet. Hebrew poetry is somewhat lost on us, but understanding the "and furthermore" nature of the couplets will deepen your understanding of the message. The whole purpose of poetry of any kind is to intensify the message.

So, there is no rhyme, but certainly, there is a meter—a rhythm caused by repetition. We have already noticed the eight repeated synonyms for God's Word. That creates a rhythm. There's more. Each verse begins with the Hebrew letter **MEM**. Why? It's poetic repetition and a memory aid.

"Above and Beyond"—*MEM*

Each of the eight verses in the Psa 119:97-104 section begins with the Hebrew letter **MEM**. This is done using only two Hebrew Words. **MA** is found twice, the attached preposition **ME** six times. Both words promote the theme. **MA** is an exclamation (e.g., "oh, how great!"). It is in the topic sentence verse and the refrain verse only. It acts as a bookend for our **MEM** section.

ME is a one-letter attached preposition (literally "from"). Hebrew often is very flexible. **ME** is such an example. It describes things distant "from" (or above) the ordinary. The **MEM** section is about all things superior or things **"above and beyond."**

The psalm is also intended to be set to music. We cannot nowadays duplicate the music or even know which instruments were used for each psalm. But we do know they did not have pianos and organs in that day. Music is powerful. It may be the only way to reach the depths of our emotions. It also helps us remember the words. This section of the Psalms is obviously meant to be remembered. Our Hymn 59 is as close as we can get in this era.

So, let's dig down and do a little verse-by-verse examination to learn the lessons given.

Verse 97 (The topic sentence)
"O how love I thy law! It is my meditation all the day."

This phrase is an exhortation to value the Word and to think about it a lot. What is the **MEM** message? **MEM** teaches us that the Word is better, superior, and above and beyond. What about this verse is above and beyond normal life? The emotion of love is a higher motivator than guilt, and the frequency is higher than if you were compelled. To the best of your ability, keep spiritual thoughts in your mind. That is the **MEM** message. Aspire to higher levels of emotion for God's Word. Think about it continually. How much should we study the Word? Five hours a day? Three? Making rules is not the way to approach the question. Let your love for the Word decide how much you meditate and on what. Let desire rule, not rules.

When I met my wife, Linda, and we fell in love, I used to be thrilled to get a letter from her. I saved them and read them multiple times. At first, I would wonder what something she wrote actually meant. But the more I got to know her, the more I understood. That includes the time she sent me an envelope full of California beach sand, as well as the time she sent me a baggie with a shark's eyeball from science class! Oh, what a sense of humor she has. No one had to force me to read those letters.

The same is true about God's Word. We read it often because we love Him. Conversely, we love Him increasingly because we read often. Our love for God's Word, and for Him, grows with thinking about His Word. So, it's circular. Love generates a desire to read continually. As we read, we increase our love for God's Word.

You may not start with loving the Word. But if you think about it continually, love will grow. Flip the switch for your own spiritual benefit. Start the engine. I hope that in your experience, you have spontaneous "Emmaus moments," where reacting to the Word makes your heart burn within you. The prodigal son parable moves me like this. The story of how Jesus responded to the woman taken in adultery moves me similarly.

Charles Spurgeon (1834-1892), a famous Baptist preacher, said this:

"I beseech you to let your Bibles be everything to you. Carry this matchless treasure with you continually and read it, and read it, and read it again and again. Turn its pages by day and by night. Let its narratives mingle with your dreams. Let its precepts color your lives; Let its promises cheer your darkness. Let its divine illumination make glad your life. As you love God, love this book. It is the book of God."

Verse 98

This is a supporting verse to the previous topic sentence. It's a **MEM** message of better results through the Scriptures.

Thou through thy commandments hast made me wiser than my enemies: for they are ever with me.

I have wondered, "Do I have enemies?" Maybe there are people who like me less than others, but surely, not enemies. I can't think of any who are out to kill me. Maybe the psalmist had these kinds of enemies.

So how valuable is this verse for me? Actually, we all have the same enemy– our propensity to sin! Our fleshly weakness, which we inherited from Adam. With this enemy, we are at war.

For we wrestle not against flesh and blood, but against principalities, against powers, against the rulers of the darkness of this world, against spiritual wickedness in high places. (Eph 6:12).

Jesus used the wisdom of the Scriptures to defeat temptation in the wilderness. He said, *"It is written"* four times during those temptations, as he quoted the Law. Spend a lot of time in Scripture, and you'll be stronger against sin. Spend a lot of time in the "wisdom" Scriptures (Psalms, Proverbs, Ecclesiastes), and when tempted, they will come to mind and strengthen you. It's our sword of the spirit, and we must arm ourselves.

What is the **MEM** message? Defense against sin comes through the Word. This statement seems like a simple statement, but if so, why are we not better at it? Are the Scriptures a way to distance ourselves **FROM** sin? Better than gritting our teeth and using raw willpower.

Verse 99

This verse is also a supporting verse to the topic sentence and another "above and beyond" benefit of time spent thinking about the Word of God.

I have more understanding than my teachers: for thy testimonies are my meditation. (v. 99).

Bible study is personal. No one can meditate on the Scriptures for you. Personal involvement is superior to passive involvement. How many days after Bible School do you remember the final points of a great class? Sometimes, but not always, things will stick with you. Because our speakers are all human beings, they sometimes say things that are not correct. The pressure is on our speakers to find new creative ideas, which can leave them out on the limb. Sometimes our teachers have "disciples," followers that are strongly disposed to accept their point of view without question.

Even barely removed from Christ's day, this was a problem.

Beloved, believe not every spirit, but try the spirits whether they are of God. Because many false prophets are gone out into the world." (1 John 4:1).

So the **MEM** lesson of this verse is that it's better to rely on your own meditations of the Word of God. I am not suggesting we should never listen to good Bible students, but do your own work. Your own meditations are more valuable to you and more retainable. When you are attending a class and you know the topic, I suggest you read up on the subject beforehand and start collecting questions.

Verse 100

I understand more than the ancients because I keep thy precepts.

Our "ancients" might be the Christadelphian "pioneers," who absolutely deserve respect. They have done much for the Truth's formation. But we are not to endorse blind acceptance of every idea. The emphasis is on the second half of the couplet. Some lessons can only be learned by experience. This verse highlights the difference between academic knowledge and life-lesson experience. The **MEM** message is obedience is above and beyond head knowledge.

There are certain skills you can only learn by experience. You can't learn to play the guitar by reading about it. Only hands-on experience will do. Similarly, who can really know what it means to *"esteem other better than themself"* (Phil 2:3) unless they truly experience this? Who can really know what it means to *"love the Lord with all your heart and soul and mind"* unless they try it? Who can know what it's like to seek *"peace with all men"* (Heb 12:14) without sacrificing one's ego? There is a cost. Every denial of sin requires the personal sacrifice of your will; you can't learn unless you try it. Counting the cost of purity is an "above and beyond" wisdom that grows with experience.

We have to try to avoid sin all the time, in all its manifestations.

> *Don't allow sin to hang around. Don't give it life. The battle against sin is an all-out war. There are not some sins that we should tolerate and make excuses for.*

Verse 101

I have refrained my feet from every evil way, that I may keep thy Word.

This is a supporting verse connected to the previous one. The ability to keep the Word comes from walking away from all evil. It turns the circle from verse 100 backward. We have to try to avoid sin **all** the time, in **all** its manifestations. This pursuit gives you "above and beyond" power in your war against evil.

> *Wherefore if thy hand or foot offend thee, cut them off, and cast them from thee, it is better for thee to enter into life halt and maimed, rather than having two hands or two feet to be cast into everlasting fire.* (Matt 18:8-9).

If you need to break a sin habit, go "cold turkey." Cut it out immediately and completely, even if you are losing something you really enjoy in your life. Don't allow sin to hang around. Don't give it life. The battle against sin is an all-out war. There are not some sins that we should tolerate and make excuses for. Paul wrote, *"make not provision for the flesh, to fulfil the lusts thereof."* (Rom 13:14).

We shouldn't pick which sins we will avoid and which we will allow. Sin kills—all of it. If you want an "above and beyond" life, pursue absolute purity in all things. It is not material to say, "Well, it's impossible, so I give up." God is merciful and honors our intentions. He is the proverbial "Father" in the prodigal son parable, eagerly waiting for us to return to Him. Your success will be "above and beyond" those who make room for their favorite sins.

Verse 102

I have not departed from thy judgments: for thou hast taught me.

This verse is the last of three verses mentioning obedience, and each adds a unique perspective. This verse emphasizes obedience as a result of the direct teaching of God. This is something we don't talk about much. Study hard and study often. Let your love for his Word move you. But God can bless your intention with a gift of knowledge. I think He participates in your spiritual growth as a partner, not promoting a lack of zeal for His Word. No laziness is allowed.

Jesus said to Peter:

> *Blessed art thou "Simon Barjona: for flesh and blood hath not revealed it unto thee, but my Father which is in heaven."* (Matt 16:17).

Howbeit when he, the Spirit of truth, is come, he will guide you into all truth: (John 16:13).

Does He do this for us when we preach? I suggest yes, but only if we load our minds with His Word first. When we open our Bible and believe God will speak to us through His Word, there is much power "above and beyond" our intellectual ability. That is the **MEM** idea—Bible understanding "above and beyond" what we could find on our own.

I have experienced this in a simple kind of process. When pondering something, I seemingly trip over just the right verse in the readings. Sometimes a good idea will pop up in my head at odd times, even at night or when I am walking. Encourage this experience. Pray for it to happen. Make room for it in your mind through meditation. Thank God for His teaching. By the way, only some things you think of this way will be correct. You will make mistakes, which you can test by the Scriptures.

The end of the Psalm 119 **MEM** section is the two-verse refrain. It's a summarizing restatement of the key ideas--a bookend or divider before the next section.

Verse 103-104

How sweet are thy words unto my taste! Yea sweeter than honey to my mouth! Through thy precepts, I get understanding: Therefore I hate every false way.

We can receive great enjoyment from Bible meditation and superior understanding to aid in the fight against evil.

There is one last important factor–prayer! The words in the canon of the Scriptures were created by inspiration, so it's safe to say these are God's Words we are reading. The psalmist addresses his poem to God. How do we know? Lots of *"thys"* in almost every verse. This **MEM** section is one affirmation prayer after another. Each of them states an intention, and the implied "Let this be true" is silently asking God to answer.

So, in an odd turn, the Psalmist is speaking words from God to God. This is the ultimate example of aligning our prayers with God's will–using His words. We sometimes allow our prayers to consist of attempts to get God to do something we want. These may not always align with what He wants. But by using Scripture promises and God's actual words, we are better in sync. Some call this "praying through Scripture," using a Scriptural citation as the content of the prayer. An example might be how Jesus used the words of Psalm 22 in his prayers on the cross.

We should want what God wants. Therefore, it is helpful to use His actual words. This is a powerful prayer technique. Use it to raise your prayer life "above and beyond."

Conclusion

My wish for you is to make God's Word your meditation, that you walk more and more in His wisdom and the powerful "above and beyond" blessings that God has for us as we truly meet in his Word.

Peter Wilson,
Verdugo Hills Ecclesia, CA

EXHORTATION AND CONSOLATION

PAUL'S ROAD TO DAMASCUS CONVERSION

By Albert Cruz

PAUL is a prominent character in the New Testament. He was the Apostle to the Gentiles and was responsible for writing much of the New Testament. A large part of the Book of Acts is devoted to Paul's work to preach the gospel message throughout the Roman world. In addition, there are many letters Paul wrote to ecclesias and to individual believers who were in those ecclesias. However, Paul started his life and religious career in a very different way.

I want to ask you to imagine a picture of two different men. The first man is a young, proud, and arrogant figure. He's a man from a noble family in Israel. He possesses the highest educational qualifications in Jewish law and traditions. He is successful, highly regarded by his peers, and destined, it seems, for the highest rabbinical position.

Our second man is old, tired, bent, and frail, a man rejected by his noble family and with few friends. His own countrymen hate him and have left him to rot in a Roman prison. Yet despite these apparent differences between the two men, and the advantage the first seems to have in every respect, the first man is frustrated, angry, and confused. He is fighting against his conscience. By contrast, the second old and tired man is at peace with himself. He is a man who rejoices in his sufferings, knowing a crown of everlasting righteousness awaits him.

Of course, you have realized these two men I have described are the same man but with totally different characters. They are Saul of Tarsus and Paul, the beloved Apostle. In Acts 22, we have Paul's account of the dramatic moment that changed his life. He was no longer one whose ambition was to be the proud, zealous "Pharisee of the Pharisees" in Israel. Now a humble, dedicated servant of Jesus Christ, the apostle to the Gentiles. We would like to spend a few moments thinking about this dramatic change of heart in Saul of Tarsus, a change which was affected by that glorious vision of the risen Christ as Saul made his way to Damascus, determined to stamp out Christianity.

Early Days

Saul of Tarsus was a Jew of the tribe of Benjamin, born in the city of Tarsus (in modern-day Turkey) but raised in Jerusalem (Phil 3:5-6, Acts 22:3). Saul's family had become citizens of Rome. So, by birth, Saul also had Roman citizenship (Acts 22:28). He was born into an eminent family of Pharisees. He trained in Biblical studies and Law under the guidance of Gamaliel (Acts 5:34; 22:3), one of the greatest and most respected rabbis of the first century. As a result, Paul had the very best education in his society. Because of his upbringing, he became fully devoted to his faith in God's Law, as a Jew, and as an eminent member of the sect of the Pharisees.

It is difficult to overestimate the influence of the sect of the Pharisees in those days. The Pharisees were a group of zealous Jews who were contemporaries of Jesus Christ. They believed they would please God by

meticulously following the Law and observing the long list of religious rules and regulations they had developed over time. Saul of Tarsus espoused this way of thinking. Despite his preeminent legal training, when Saul of Tarsus could not refute the preaching of Stephen, a man without his education in the Law, he became arrogant, bitter, and angry. He couldn't accept the truthful and wholesome words of Stephen. This is the portrait of Saul of Tarsus, carnally minded, hardened, proud, and angry!

Other Plans for Saul

No one possessed the power to change Saul but our Lord Jesus Christ! It required a true conversion to the mind and teaching of Christ, like Peter, who, after three years with the Lord, was told, *"when you are converted strengthen your brethren."* (Luke 22:31-32) We also should also understand in our hearts the meaning of true conversion (Matt 13:15). True conversion may not come immediately after baptism. It can come much later, just like Peter and the disciples. Saul of Tarsus had heard and known of the teaching of the gospel before his Damascus conversion. Saul was just so stubborn that he refused to accept the Master's teaching.

However, God had other plans for Saul. Along that road to Damascus, the resurrected Jesus appeared to Saul and questioned why he was persecuting him and his followers. Saul responded, *"What shall I do, Lord?"* (Acts 22:10 ESV). Saul, though he had an incorrect understanding of what was happening in the religious climate of his time, was a sincerely devout man dedicated to serving God. Therefore, when Jesus confronted him on the road to Damascus, Saul's heart was ready to be changed. This recognition of his own failings did not cause him to despair or become preoccupied with his weakness. He realized God's love and mercy were far greater than his shortcomings and sin.

What About Us?

So, there is a lesson for us, brothers and sisters. Paul always looked to the future, though he never forgot his past. His bitter persecution of the ecclesia, and his hand in the murder of Stephen and Christ's followers, did not paralyze him with self-pity but caused him to acknowledge his failings (1 Cor 15:9).

As we partake of the emblems, we also are exhorted to reflect upon our past life. Suppose our examination is really an honest one. In that case, we too will acknowledge the flaws in our character, words, thoughts, and actions and commit to rededicating ourselves to follow the Master's example.

Our conversion will never be as dramatic as Paul's. But each week, we must be converted, little by little. The task of being converted from a sinner to a saint is not the work of a moment in the waters of baptism. It's the work of a lifetime! We must slowly convert the mind of the flesh to developing the mind of the spirit. But if we can achieve that transition, what joy awaits us!

Albert Cruz,
Quezon City Ecclesia, Philippines

MUSIC AND PRAISE

HOW CAN I, EVEN I, BE CREATIVE?

By Nathan Richard

WHO comes to mind when you think of a creative person? What are the characteristics of this individual—outrageously artistic? Flamboyantly energetic, fantastically extroverted, and full of endless thoughts and ideas? Bursting at the seams with musicality, humming and doodling without any cares in the world? Slightly out of touch with reality, with their head oftentimes in the clouds?

Well, that's not me.

I'm at home in a world of spreadsheets. I quickly become bored and impatient when listening to grandiose ideas, immediately spotting the impracticalities. I spend most of each day in a manufacturing plant, implementing and encouraging ideas (not generating them myself). I'm naturally introverted and driven by rational reasoning to a fault. And I have never been accused of wearing my emotions on my sleeve! Yet at the same time, I consider myself to be a creative individual. Those who hear me play the piano on Sunday morning may be shocked at my lack of stereotypical "creative" personality traits.

Musical Creative Process

Although one can (and should) argue that creativity towards the glory of God occurs in all aspects of our lives, my primary creative lens has been through music. To demonstrate what creativity as a form of praise looks like from the perspective of an overly rational creator, let's examine how I create music as a pianist and as a composer.

My creative process as a pianist reflects my natural tendencies toward logic and rational problem-solving. Practicing scales and arpeggios for hours on end is far from artistically invigorating, and much of my piano practice revolves around solving very specific technical or musical problems. If I am playing a melody in octaves, should I highlight the lower or higher note? If the music requires a trill or embellishment, where is the balance or center of gravity in my hand and fingers that provide a light and articulate touch?

Similarly, here's an example of my iterative process when arranging a solo piano setting to a hymn from the 2002 Christadelphian Hymn Book, #168, *The Lord Is In His Holy Temple*. The music starts as a simple sketch, with a harmonic progression penciled in. This is derived primarily via music theory through various trials and errors.

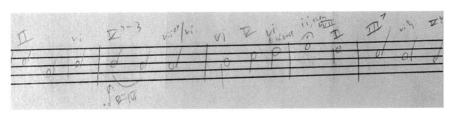

Next, a more detailed sketch is created, including inner voices and potential rhythms.

Then the hard work of editing and revising begins. The music is typed up and corrected while at the piano bench to better achieve the intended musical objectives, such as:
- A clear and recognizable melody,
- Music matching the text, climaxing on "let all of the earth" and diminishing through "be silent before Him."

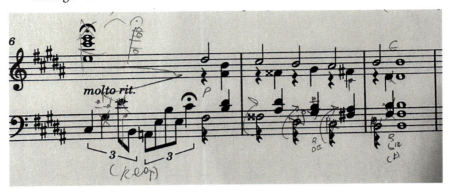

And this finally results in a finished product!

Diversity in Unity

While I personally approach music creation in this method, there are numerous different creative approaches to composition. Looking through music history, a composer such as J.S. Bach achieved virtual mathematical perfection in his counterpoint. For a fun rabbit hole, take a look at his *Musical Offering* or *Art of the Fugue*.

Bach could take a brutally difficult theme and turn it literally inside out, backward, and upside down—all at the same time.

Other composers such as Wolfgang Amadeus Mozart or Franz Schubert seemed to fit the prototypical "creative genius" description, where their compositions flow from an inner voice as indicated by their first draft being nearly identical to the published work. By contrast, composers such as Ludwig van Beethoven or Johannes Brahms spent years tinkering with their themes, working through each note and phrase until the composer was 100% satisfied.

The beauty of this diversity in creativity is that it enables different individuals with unique personalities and characteristics to contribute in their own creative way. This diversity is good! We see this in the various personalities displayed by different Biblical characters: Paul's legal arguments, Peter's impulsive zeal, Isaac's empathy and relationship building, David's sweeping emotions, and Ezra's studiousness.

This ultimately speaks to the diversity that God has designed within the unity of the body of Christ. **Each of us can offer our creativity towards furthering God's glory, no matter our personality!** Just because I approach creation with a methodical approach does not diminish the person who can spontaneously improvise a new song or someone who works best in a collaborative setting. These different approaches yield different creations that all speak to the multifaceted character and glory of God.

As the seminal 1 Corinthians 12 passage discusses, *"for even as the body is one and yet has many members, and all the members of the body, though they are many, are one body, so also is Christ."* (1 Cor 12:12).[1] We are all created by God in His image, and the uniqueness of every person speaks to God's creativity and the different roles that each of us fulfills in our walk. When put together, the sum of the whole body exceeds the individual contributions of each part.

Amazingly, the same God who made the beautiful mountains of the Pacific Northwest is the same God who designed our universe's chemical structures and molecular bonds. He is also the same Creator of the linguistic, anthropological, and sociological factors that have led to countless unique communities across the history of the world. As God Himself is a diverse and creative being, we are likewise all called to be creative in our unique ways, doing all to the glory of God (1 Cor 10:31, Col 3:17). Some potential examples include:

- A parent creating a fun craft to encourage a child's imagination.
- A computer programmer elegantly solving a specific coding challenge.
- A student seizing an opportunity in a study group's conversation to add a Biblical connection.
- A homeowner using common materials to solve an uncommon problem.
- A retail worker engaging reluctant customers in an unexpectedly positive and vibrant discussion.
- A Bible student presenting a lesson with a unique introduction or a fascinating twist to better connect with an audience.

It is in God's nature and character to be a Creator. This truth leaps from the Scriptures from the very start. *"In the beginning God created."* (Gen 1:1). Only a few paragraphs later, God's first words to humanity were to *"be fruitful and multiply."* (Gen 1:28). While this commandment is nuanced with many applications, the concept of being fruitful implies creating new things, just as fruit springs forth from a branch. We are called to create new life, as God emphasizes the need for humans to be creative from the very beginning of God's plan. We are created in God's image, and as images of God, we reflect God's character. Therefore just as God is a Creator, we too must reflect the creativity that is a crucial part of God Himself.

We see this focus extend throughout the Bible, culminating in God's final Master Plan for the earth to *"be filled with the knowledge of the glory of the LORD, as the waters cover the sea."* (Hab 2:14). As we exercise our creativity, we manifest God's creativity as the Creator of the world.

Messiness of Creativity

Speaking on behalf of the "non-creative" personalities, one common pitfall is a fear of failure. Perhaps you, like me, pursue perfection and shy away from opportunities with a high degree of risk. I naturally prefer life to be black-and-white and avoid situations with uncertainty.

Our calling to be creative, however, requires embracing shades of gray. Creativity is messy and is never guaranteed to lead to the outcomes we originally intended. What we create is not perfect! *"There is nothing new under the sun"* (Eccl 1:9), so as images of God, we only reflect the creative nature that God has. We ourselves do not create new creations.

Looking at the previously mentioned composition, for instance, I remain unsatisfied with the final product! The concluding section lacks momentum and has a texture that is too thin, leading to a climax that does not quite land the knockout punch and falls just short. I love elements of this composition, but creativity requires us to embrace our shortcomings. Pursuing perfectionism can lead to paralysis, an inability ever to begin creating. At its root, this is an exercise in legalism and human pride, an inability to rely on God's grace to cover our inadequacies as we attempt to produce work that is "good enough," attempting to have our works be sufficient.

Extending this further, a fascinating phenomenon occurs in a Conservatory setting. After being surrounded by a musical environment for several months, many students find their ears improve faster than their musical abilities. When listening to identical recordings six months apart, students can critique the music much more quickly, accurately, and comprehensively than before. In my case, this meant that in high school, I thought I was God's greatest gift to the piano, and I could do no wrong. Yet now, when I listen back on my high school recordings, I cringe as I hear my flaws, following a musical maturation process where I gained insight and clarity into how far my piano playing was from the ideal musical outcome. This phenomenon often causes a miniature crisis for Conservatory students as they realize, "Oh no, I'm not anywhere close to being as good as I thought I was. I have so much to learn!"

And does this not mirror our experience as maturing followers of Christ? The Law was introduced to bring awareness of sin (Rom 3:20), sharpening our focus on our shortcomings. The purpose of the Law was not to overcome sin via our personal piety and adherence to it but to teach us our efforts are insufficient and fall short. This points to our need for Christ's redeeming and atoning work (Gal 3:24).

Therefore, as we grow in faith, our "musical ear" is sharpened. We recognize nuances and unexpected challenges of living a spiritual life we never realized we were missing. Growing in faith provides us with better knowledge of the ideal way to live, as embodied by Christ (Col 1:26-2:3). Instead of our deeper knowledge increasing our pride, this fuller understanding of our weaknesses leads us towards **more** faith, towards **more** humility, towards **more** reliance on Jesus as we become **more** aware of our sin and our need for Christ (we see this played out in John 8:5-9 and expounded in 1 Cor 1:18-31).

Being creative is not an easy commission from God. Yet, He gives us this command to show how much we ultimately need Him. We cannot create perfection of our own accord. Our creations fall short of the perfect glory only God can create. Instead, our creativity is an outpouring of our desire to manifest God's nature in our uniquely created way while simultaneously reminding us that Christ's *"power is perfected in weakness."* (2 Cor. 12:9). It is ultimately not about our own personality, talents, or work ethic that manifests God's glory. That honor belongs to Christ, who covers our imperfections and presents us as holy, blameless, and beyond reproach to God (Col 1:22). We are **all** designed to be creative and glorify and praise God through our modest creations.

Nathan Richard,
Chicago Ecclesia, IL

[1] All Biblical quotations are from the NASB translation.
[2] Bro. Nathan Richard can be contacted at nwrichard3@gmail.com.

Want to hear Nathan's completed (yet imperfect!) arrangement of *"The Lord is in His Holy Temple"*?

Visit mytidings.org/h9b to listen!

EXPOSITION

PART 4
GOD IS NOT A MONSTER

GOD'S JEALOUSY

By Chris Sales

IN our article we looked at God's attitude toward women. We saw the laws surrounding the treatment of women in the Old Testament were there to control and regulate a "fallen human" problem–not idealize it or condone it! God is not misogynistic, but instead loves and values women greatly!

In this article, we will take a closer look at the question of whether the God of the Bible is a jealous God and whether or not His demand for praise and sacrifices is due to His arrogance and need for affirmation from His creation!

We begin by asking the question: Is jealousy always a bad thing? Think about it.

Jealousy that is prompted when others use our possessions or are friendly with our friends can cause selfishness or insecurity. However, jealousy can also be provoked by deep love!

A husband or wife who does not feel jealous or angry when another flirts with their spouse may not be fully committed to the marriage relationship, or they may feel secure in the relationship and trust their husband or wife implicitly. Likewise, if a married person treasures their spouse, they will guard their relationship with all they have and not deliberately cause the other to feel jealousy. If they do not, the other half may rightly feel they are not cared for.

The Apostle Paul was inspired to write, *"I am jealous for you with a godly jealousy. I promised you to one husband, to Christ, so that I might present you as a pure virgin to him."* (2 Cor 11:2)[1] This is how Paul felt about the believers in Corinth! His jealousy was due to his deep love for his spiritual brothers and sisters, not hurt, pride, or selfishness. This is how the Bible defines "godly jealousy."

God felt this way about Israel in the Old Testament. He committed Himself as a loving husband and expected the same in return from the people He treasured. In the context of His strong feelings for His people, despite their unfaithfulness, God passionately says: *"My heart is changed within me; all my compassion is aroused."* (Hos 11:8).

In Isaiah 54:5 (KJV), we read, *"For thy Maker is thine husband; the LORD of hosts is his name; and thy Redeemer the Holy One of Israel; The God of the whole earth shall he be called."*

And Jeremiah 31:32 (KJV) says, *"which my covenant they brake, although I was an husband unto them, saith the LORD."*

God's strong feelings toward His people were like a young person's emotions toward a new spouse. As is said in Jeremiah 2:2 (NET), *"This is what the LORD says: 'I have fond memories of you, how devoted you were to me in your early years. I remember how you loved me like a new bride.'"*

We see then that God often responds like a wounded lover, reluctant to bring judgment, for Israel specifically, and all His people ultimately! He demonstrates patience and love—only reacting with divine jealousy and anger when provoked beyond measure or when He is fearful for His beloved's best interest.

Feel the emotion when God agonizingly says in Ezekiel 6:9, *"They will [eventually] realize how I was crushed by their unfaithful heart that turned from me and by their eyes that lusted after idols."*

For example, we may read about the incident of the golden calf in a detached way and feel surprised at God's strong reaction to the people's idolatry. But, since Israel had just pledged their allegiance to God and had promised to serve only Him, it would be like a newly married person finding their spouse in bed with someone else on their honeymoon!

God is not some immaterial entity or impersonal being, as some people think He should be. He is not a computer program or super intelligent AI system dispassionately running the universe. God is an engaging, personal being who connects with humankind. He is looking for a reciprocal relationship with us! That relationship is so important to Him and so necessary for our well-being that He guards it jealously.

God knew that worshiping idols would lead His people to moral perversion. Idol worship generally involved some sort of immorality, child sacrifice, violence, or at the very least, undermined God's authority. God knew it would result in not only a rejection of His principles and the moral standards that held the society together but, more importantly, a spiritual breakdown that would affect their eternal salvation.

God wants us all to participate in His promised, incredible eternal future. Idol worship will lead His beloved to eternal death. It is like a husband or wife watching their spouse being seduced by a villain. Of course, they will jealously guard them against an imposter they know will harm them. But even then, God's jealous reaction is an attempt to win over His people! He still loves them and would take them back, despite their unfaithfulness!

He says in Ezekiel 18:30-32 (NET):

> *Therefore, I will judge each person according to his conduct, O house of Israel, declares the Sovereign Lord. Repent and turn from all your wickedness; then it will not be an obstacle leading to iniquity. Throw away all your sins you have committed and fashion yourselves a new heart and a new spirit! Why should you die, O house of Israel? For I take no delight in the death of anyone, declares the Sovereign Lord. Repent and live!*

God's jealousy implies vulnerability and the capacity to experience pain. He is not a petty, power-hungry deity obsessed with dominating people! In fact, God gets jealous precisely because He cares and loves His people deeply!

God gets jealous of our best interests, and His commandments are given for our good. It is only self-harm when we live selfishly and create our gods in our own images, living as if nothing is beyond our tiny mortal existence. Most importantly, we lose the precious opportunity to share in the glorious future God has promised to those who love Him and keep His commandments.

Noted author C.S. Lewis (1898-1963) commented on the smallness of our perspective compared to the vastness of God's. He described how that relates to our obsession with idolatry in all its forms and God's jealous reaction to our shortsightedness:

> "If we consider the unblushing promises of reward and the staggering nature of the rewards promised in the Gospels, it would seem that our Lord finds our desires, not too strong, but too weak. We are half-hearted creatures, fooling about with drink, and sex, and ambition when infinite joy is offered us, like an ignorant child who wants to go on making mud pies in a slum because he cannot imagine what is

meant by the offer of a holiday at sea. We are far too easily pleased."[2]

We see the same kind of jealousy for the things of God when Jesus overturned the tables of the money changers, driving the merchants out of the Temple. Many observers may have thought Jesus was overreacting and out of control. But the disciples recalled another verse that is helpful in our discussion in this article: *"Zeal for Your house has eaten Me up."* (John 2:17 NKJV). Jesus would allow all kinds of abuse to be heaped on him. Still, when his Father's house was mistreated, the righteous anger born from jealousy burned in him. His anger showed how much he cared for his own people, as well as the Gentiles, whose courtyard had been turned into a marketplace!

So, given that God is a jealous and passionate God and His son, the Lord Jesus Christ, displays the same emotion and love, is it wrong or inappropriate for God to require praise, admiration, and devotion? Is He, as the New Atheists would have us believe, a power-hungry, maniacal, arrogant being? Nothing could be further from the truth! On the contrary, we see the God of the Bible as a humble, self-giving Being, focused on the needs of others. Jesus perfectly manifested these characteristics in his life, death, and resurrection.

The true nature of pride and humility can perhaps best be seen in the incident of the washing of the disciples' feet. At this time, Jesus *"knew that the Father had put all things under his power"* (John 13:3), and yet he *"got up from the meal, took off his outer clothing, and wrapped a towel around his waist. After that, he poured water into a basin and began to wash his disciples' feet, drying them with the towel that was wrapped around him."* (vv. 4-5). It was a choice to serve, despite his superior position. This is true humility— having the power to serve.

False humility, which is actually disguised pride, is seen in Peter's reaction to the Lord's service: *"Lord, are you going to wash my feet?"* (v. 6). Jesus gently rebukes him and then reminds all the disciples:

> Do you understand what I have done for you? You call me 'Teacher' and 'Lord,' and rightly so, for that is what I am. Now that I, your Lord and Teacher, have washed your feet, you also should wash one another's feet. I have set you an example that you should do as I have done for you. Very truly I tell you, no servant

is greater than his master, nor is a messenger greater than the one who sent him. Now that you know these things, you will be blessed if you do them. (vv. 12-17).

What more appropriate response could there be than to honor and glorify such a Lord and Master? *"Worthy is the Lamb, who was slain, to receive power and wealth and wisdom and strength and honor and glory and praise!"* (Rev 5:12). How much more his Father? God is God and worthy of all praise. He does not mandate praise, like an egotistical dictator that rules with an iron fist and mandates obedience. Rather, the natural reaction of anyone who truly appreciates all that God has done for us, His love, and the sacrifices He made so we can have abundant life, is to acknowledge how much He deserves praise and worship of the highest order!

You are worthy, our Lord and God, to receive glory and honor and power, for you created all things, and by your will they were created and have their being. (Rev 4:11).

In our next (and last) article, we hope to examine the topic of God and genocide.

*Chris Sales,
Collingwood Ecclesia, ON*

---

[1] AllAll Scriptural citations are taken from the New International Version, unless specifically noted.
[2] Lewis, C.S., "The Weight of Glory," in *The Weight of Glory and Other Addresses*, New York, HarperOne, 2001, Page 26

The natural reaction of anyone who truly appreciates all that God has done for us, His love, and the sacrifices He made so we can have abundant life, is to acknowledge how much He deserves praise and worship of the highest order!

FIRST PRINCIPLES

PART 3
THE RIGHTEOUS SHALL LIVE BY FAITH

By Richard Morgan

LAST month we had a look at the origin of the phrase "the righteous shall live by faith"[1] found in Habakkuk 2:4. These words are quoted three times in the New Testament, in Romans, Galatians, and Hebrews. Each time there is an emphasis on a different word. In Romans, the book about the righteousness of God, we learn that the *"righteous"* shall live by faith. In Galatians, Paul is concerned with contrasting faith with law, so in quoting Habakkuk he tells us the righteous shall live by *"faith."* Finally, in Hebrews, the quotation occurs just before the honor roll of the faithful in chapter 11, who all

tidings.org

45

lived by faith—so Hebrews emphasizes the point that the righteous shall *"live"* by faith.

For our consideration in this article, we're going to have a look at the context of the words found in Romans. They appear in Paul's thesis statement:

> For I am not ashamed of the gospel, for it is the power of God for salvation to everyone who believes, to the Jew first and also to the Greek. For in it the righteousness of God is revealed from faith for faith, as it is written, "The righteous shall live by faith." (Rom 1:16-17).

Paul tells us that Habakkuk's words reveal the righteousness of God; but what **is** God's righteousness? A useful exercise is to peruse the many passages in the Old Testament that explain God's righteousness, and typically we find passages like this one from Psalm 143:1-2:

> Hear my prayer, O Lord; give ear to my pleas for mercy! In your faithfulness answer me, in your righteousness! Enter not into judgment with your servant, for no one living is righteous before you.

Notice the words in verse 1 where righteousness is paired with faithfulness. David's prayer is that God's righteousness will be revealed by Him being faithful to his servant, and we find that to be a constant theme throughout the Bible. God exhibits his righteousness in the way he treats others, centering on his faithfulness, a characteristic at the very center of God's description of his glory found in Exodus 34 which I have set out in its chiastic form below from Exodus 34:6-7:

> The Lord passed before him and proclaimed, "The Lord, the Lord, a God
>
> **A** *merciful and gracious, slow to anger,*
>
> **B** *and abounding in steadfast love*
>
> **C** *and faithfulness,*
>
> **B** *keeping steadfast love for thousands,*
>
> **A** *forgiving iniquity and transgression and sin, but who will by no means clear the guilty."*

Faithfulness is God's rock-like attribute of reliability and trustworthiness. And it's because we can rely on God we can have faith in Him. Or to put it another way, we can have faith in God's faithfulness.

This helps explain what Paul means in the passage from Romans cited above—*"the righteousness of God is revealed from faith for faith."* What does *"from faith for faith"* mean?

First, notice the exact wording of our key phrase from Habakkuk 2:4—*"The righteous shall live by his faith."* When quoted in the New Testament, the pronoun "his" is missing each time, including here in Romans. However, there's some ambiguity in the fact the Septuagint, which would have been the common version read in the first century, reads *"The just shall live by my faith,"* meaning God's faith. Paul's version with no pronoun leaves the question open whether he is quoting the Hebrew or Greek text.

However, perhaps what we have here is a designed ambiguity. What if Paul wants us to understand that our faith and God's faith (or faithfulness) work together? It's about our faith manifested in us trusting in God's faithfulness, hence Paul's *"from faith for faith"*— or to put it another way, "from God's faithfulness for our faith."

Considering this, it's interesting to note that in Romans 3, Paul says **God is also justified by faith!** In verse 3, he writes, *"What if some were unfaithful? Does their faithlessness nullify the faithfulness of God?"* God's faithfulness cannot be upset by the fact that the Jewish people were unfaithful; God remains trustworthy. Then he says, *"By no means! Let God be true though every one were a liar, as it is written, 'That you may be justified in your words, and prevail when you are judged.'"* (v. 4). So, God is justified in his actions by virtue of his continuing faithfulness. This principle is a theme that runs through Romans, which, like Habakkuk, considers the problem of theodicy— the righteousness of God in the midst of an evil world.

Later in Romans 3:21-22, Paul writes, *"the righteousness of God has been manifested... the righteousness of God through faith in Jesus Christ."* That righteousness is seen in God forgiving people for their sins, or in the words of verses 24-25 *"justified by his grace as a gift, through the redemption that is in Christ Jesus, whom God put forward as a propitiation by his blood, to be received by faith. This was to show God's righteousness."* What these words tell us is that God's righteousness is revealed by him being faithful to those in covenant relationship with him. He will forgive them for their sins.

What we also see in these words is the faithfulness of God manifest in his son. The phrase in verse 22—*"through faith in Jesus Christ,"* is rendered in the NET Bible as *"through the faithfulness of Jesus Christ."* Whether it's God's faithfulness, or it being manifest in His son, our faith depends on God being true to His servants and forgiving us for our sins.

Sometimes the concepts Paul outlines in Romans are a little hard to understand, so let's look at an example that Paul uses hidden beneath the surface of the text.

Back in chapter 1, in his introductory words, Paul says his treatise is *"concerning his Son, who was descended from David according to the flesh."* (v. 3). Why David? Because he is the prime example Paul uses to demonstrate God's righteousness, faithfulness, and the forgiveness of sins.

Look again at chapter 3 and notice how many times Paul quotes David. Verse 4, for instance, is a direct quotation from Psalm 51:

To the choirmaster. A Psalm of David, when Nathan the prophet went to him, after he had gone in to Bathsheba. Have mercy on me, O God, according to your steadfast love; according to your abundant mercy blot out my transgressions. Against you, you only, have I sinned and done what is evil in your sight, so that you may be justified in your words and blameless in your judgment. (Psa 51:1-4).

Here is David trusting—or having faith—in God's character of mercy and steadfast love. Then, another of David's psalms is quoted at the end of this section in Romans in chapter 4:6-8:

> Blessed is the one whose transgression is forgiven, whose sin is covered. Blessed is the man against whom the Lord counts no iniquity, and in whose spirit there is no deceit. (Psa. 32:1-2).

David wrote both psalms at the time of his sin with Bathsheba, and so we have here a powerful example of God's faithfulness to his servant despite his sin and the forgiveness he was willing to offer.

There's another quotation from a psalm of David in between these two, which forms a pivot in the text. Verse 20 says, *"For by works of the law no human being will be justified in his sight,"* words which come from Psalm 143:2. Remember, this is the psalm we opened with where David cries to God in the first verse *"In your faithfulness answer me, in your righteousness!"*

With these words of David, and example of his forgiveness, in mind, notice the structure of the text is that of a courtroom scene:

- Rom 3:9—accusation: all have sinned.
- Rom 3:10-18—evidence: Scriptural testimony.
- Rom 3:19—verdict: guilty.
- Rom 3:24—sentence: forgiveness.

David understood this. He was accused by Nathan and the evidence was overwhelming–he had sinned by committing adultery and murder. But whereas the Law would have sentenced him to death, God forgave him for his sin.

Back in chapter 1, Paul gives us a list of sins, ending the list with the words *"Those who practice such things deserve to die"* (v. 32), something which was true for David concerning his sin with Bathsheba. However, in using these words, it is possible Paul is quoting David after the prophet Nathan confronted him regarding his sin. After hearing the parable, Nathan told him about the rich man who stole the poor man's lamb, David said, *"The man who has done this deserves to die"* (2 Sam. 12:5) and in saying those words, David indicted himself.

The next thing Paul writes in Romans, at the beginning of chapter 2, also alludes to this event in David's life. Paul says, *"You have no excuse, O man, everyone one of you who judges. For in passing judgment on another you condemn yourself, because you, the judge, practice the very same things"* (v1), echoing Nathan's *"You are the man!"* (2 Sam 12:7).

We're talking here about the man after God's heart—the otherwise immensely faithful David. And if we are honest with ourselves, when we read that list of sins in Romans 1, we realize we are guilty too, something Paul concludes in chapter 3 saying, *"All, both Jews and Greeks, are under sin"* (v. 9).

He then follows, Romans 3:10-18 with a list of evidence from the Old Testament, the story of human beings replete with sin throughout history. If you look carefully at the list of quotations in this passage, you'll notice that most of them are from the psalms, and they're all psalms of David. So, once again, Paul is quoting the man after God's heart. But he does so in a most intriguing way. For instance, the words "*The venom of asps is under their lips*" (v. 13) is a quotation from Psalm 140:3—"*under their lips is the venom of asps.*" David wrote this psalm against sinners he encountered in his life. But if we carry on reading the very next verse of the psalm, we encounter the words, "*Guard me, O LORD, from the hands of the wicked; preserve me from violent men, who have planned to trip up my feet.*" Who was it who planned to trip up Uriah's feet to hide his sin? David! Here is an example of a man who judged sinners in his words but in practicing the same things, condemned himself.

We find the same phenomenon in the other quotations. Romans 3:14 says, "*Their mouth is full of curses and bitterness,*" a quotation from Psalm 10:7—"*His mouth is filled with cursing and deceit.*" Again, read the next verse and see that David indicted himself– "*He sits in ambush in the villages; in hiding places he murders the innocent,*" something David did to Uriah.

One more example will suffice to illustrate what Paul is doing with these quotations. Romans 3:18 says, "*There is no fear of God before their eyes*" which comes from Psalm 36:1—"*there is no fear of God before his eyes,*" which follow with the words in verse 2, "*For he flatters himself in his own eyes that his iniquity cannot be found out and hated,*" something, again, David thought in trying to cover up his sin.

The fundamental principle Paul hammers home by using the example of David is "*All have sinned and fall short of the glory of God.*" (Rom 3:23).

However, God forgave David. Why? Perhaps there's an answer in some more words of David that he spoke to Saul when he spared his life:

The LORD rewards every man for his righteousness and his faithfulness, for the Lord gave you into my hand today, and I would not put out my hand against the Lord's anointed. 24 Behold, as your life was precious this day in my sight, so may my life be precious in the sight of the Lord, and may he deliver me out of all tribulation. (1 Sam 26:23-24).

Here David invokes words memorialized in another of his psalms—"*With the merciful you show yourself merciful.*" (Psa 18:25). David, despite his mistakes, was a man of high godly character. As a man after God's heart, he was merciful just as God is merciful. As David spared Saul's life, so God spared his. And in this passage from 1 Samuel, we find the central theme of the righteous living by faith in David's words *"The LORD rewards every man for his righteousness and his faithfulness."*

Richard Morgan,
Simi Hills Ecclesia, CA

---

[1] All Scriptural citations are taken from the English Standard Version, unless otherwise noted.

LETTERS TO THE EDITOR

THE PRAYER THAT GOD ALWAYS ANSWERS IN THE AFFIRMATIVE

In a recent article, *"We Do Not Know What We Ought To Pray For"* (February 2023) in the Prayer series, Darren Tappouras wrestles with several passages that plainly tell us that God grants you whatsoever you ask.

The contexts of these seeming *carte blanche* passages point to a solution that leaves no vexation. Yes, God does give whatever you ask for, as long as you understand that the "whatever" refers to "whatever sin you ask forgiveness for."

Jesus' statement, as recorded in Mark, is plainly in the context of forgiveness:

> Therefore I tell you, whatever you ask in prayer, believe that you have received it, and it will be yours. And whenever you stand praying, forgive, if you have anything against anyone, so that your Father also who is in heaven may forgive you your trespasses. *(*Mark 11:24-25 ESV).

The conjunctive *"and"* at the beginning of v. 25 indicates a direct connection between the two statements. The phrase *"whenever you stand praying"* is, therefore, to be understood as "whenever you stand praying for forgiveness for your trespasses." Thus, *"whatever you ask in prayer"* is "whatever sins you ask to be forgiven."

This is the same message as in the Lord's Prayer (Matt 6:14-15). God forgives whatsoever we ask, provided we also grant the same to those who cause us harm—whatever it might be.

The four similar statements Jesus made in his final address to the disciples (John 14:13-14; 15:7, 16; 16:23) are also in the context of forgiveness of sins, though not as plainly stated. These passages are all associated with the coming of the Comforter (Helper in the ESV), Counselor (NIV), and Greek *parakletos*. The Comforter is identified by John himself as the resurrected Jesus, the propitiator of our sins. *"But if anyone does sin, we have an advocate [parakletos] with the Father, Jesus Christ the righteous."* (I John 2:1-2). This is the only other place in the New Testament where *parakletos* appears. Again the context is forgiveness of sins.

Another passage that bears directly on this subject is Paul preaching in the synagogue of Antioch of Pisidia. He tells the audience, *"through this man* [Jesus] *forgiveness of sins is proclaimed to you, and by him* **everyone** *who believes is freed from* **everything** *which you could not be freed by the law of Moses."* (Acts 13:38-39).

Do not diminish the universality of *"whatever we ask in prayer, God will grant,"* but do interpret this in context. We all have all of our sins forgiven, whatever they are. These are the prayers that God always answers "Yes."

David Levin,
Denver Ecclesia, CO

AUTHOR RESPONSE

Bro. David Levin's proposal is quite sound, and we are in total agreement that the only valid response from God in these prayer guarantees is "yes."

Therefore, we need to narrow the scope somehow to determine just what they are referring to. Bro. David's proposal that they refer to God forgiving our sins is very encouraging.

As foremost and as central, forgiveness is as an essential element in the "indescribable gift" of God. May I suggest that not only is forgiveness of sins in scope here but also included is the power to overcome sin in our life through faith.

For example, the immediate context of the prayer guarantee in John 15:16 is that the disciple is chosen for the objective to *"bear fruit"* and this is illustrated in verse 17 as to *"love one another."*

> I chose you and appointed you so that you might go and bear fruit--fruit that will last--and so that whatever you ask in my name the Father will give you. This is my command: Love each other. (NIV).

Sin in our life is dealt with by God both through forgiveness (justification) and the empowerment and motivation to develop a life of holiness (sanctification). God's power to achieve both these objectives appears to me to be on offer here.

The multidimensional aspect of the guarantee is illustrated in Matthew 7:7, which tells us to ask–seek–knock. God's response promised is that we will receive—find—open. Seeking and knocking would suggest a lifetime of growth and spiritual development.

Also, the use of the plural gift responses in the guarantee—*"things"* (Mark 11:24), *"Whatever"* (Matt 21:22, 1 John 3:22 (KJV), John 14:13), *"anything"* (1 John 5:14), and *"good gifts"* (Matt 7:11), may well be referring to different types of sins or multiple sin events. Still, to me, they seem to imply that God's prayer guarantees not only to grant us the incredible gift of forgiveness but if we ask in faith and true commitment (Jas 1:5-6), His power is there to help us overcome sin in our lives.

Darren Tappouras,
Gosford Ecclesia, NSW

THE HOUSE OF PRAYER FOR ALL NATIONS

I have enjoyed reading *The Tidings* for many years and appreciate the spiritual tone of the magazine, the current volume being no exception. However, I feel that in regard to the contents of Bro. George Booker's article dealing with The Temple of Ezekiel's Prophecy, and Bro. Sulley's presentation of it should be balanced out. The last nine chapters of Ezekiel are a substantial and tangible part of the Bible.

I appreciate that for many years the matter has been one of differing opinions on the nature, size, and shape of the Temple outlined therein. The subject is not an essential doctrine to be believed, which should not affect fellowship, and I believe that when we appear before the Judgment Seat, we will not be judged on our opinion on the matter, but rather why we held that opinion, and what we did with that belief.

While Bro. Roberts clearly expressed that, in his opinion, it was not an essential doctrine to be believed, he wrote the following in *"Thirteen Lectures on The Apocalypse"*:

> "God himself is the Temple of the people who compose it. But we should make a mistake in supposing that because this symbolic city has no temple, therefore the Temple exhibited to Ezekiel as the central pivot of the glorious government machinery of the future age will not have a literal existence. There is a place for every truth. What is true of the symbolic New Jerusalem is no guide to the truths concerning the literal arrangements of the kingdom of God. This we must seek at other sources, which are very abundant and very clear."

Bro. John Carter, in *The Letter to the Hebrews* (Page 167), writes:

> "The Holy City is called "Jerusalem which is above." That does not mean that it is in heaven. It is Jerusalem, the exalted, upon earth. At the same time the figurative meaning, based upon and never dissociated from the literal, must not be lost sight of. But the Lamb and his bride are inseparably associated with Mount Zion topographically, that being their capital city."

He continues (on page 172),

> "God treats His house as one in all ages. He asked them, Who is left among you that saw this house in her first glory? and He spake although the house had been completely overthrown and that was a new building. The temple overthrown was one with that rebuilt. And for nigh 2000 years there has been no temple of the Lord; but the Branch shall build the temple of the Lord, and the temple will be the same house in God's view. Of that He says "The latter glory of this house shall be greater than the former." (Hag.2:9).

In the Book of Hebrews 13:9, Paul is speaking to his countrymen, *"For it is a good thing that the heart be established with grace, not with meats which have not profited them that have been occupied therein."* Grace here stands for the way of life in Christ; *"meats"* for the observance of the ritual of the law, which was unprofitable. The unprofitableness is next illustrated, *"We have an altar whereof they have no right to eat which serve the tabernacle."* (Heb 13:10).

The writer and readers were Hebrew. And it is from this standpoint that we must approach the questions. Who are we? What is the altar? And what is the tabernacle? The "we" in this case is "we Hebrews." It is evident that by the altar, he means sacrifice.

Bro. Carter also wrote, "The Tabernacle is that described in the Law of Moses, UPON WHICH ALL THE REASONING IN THE EPISTLE HAS BEEN BASED. The Temple of later days is not considered, the whole argument being founded upon the original commandments given to Moses, concerning both structure and service." (Page 177).

No doubt there is a secondary application to believers of all ages, but we should bear in mind the apostle's original purpose of writing.

"For the bodies of those beasts, whose blood is brought into the sanctuary by the high priest for sin, are burnt without the camp." (Heb.13:11.) The allusion is to the Day of Atonement, described in Leviticus 16.

Isaiah 56:7 (NKJV) tells us, *"My house shall be called a house of prayer for all nations."* This house, like the Tabernacle and the Temple of Solomon, is of a Divine pattern (Ezek 40-48).

Christ himself confirmed, *"Is it not written, My house shall be called of all nations the house of prayer?"* (Mark 11:17). The Lord here quotes from Zechariah 14:16, the *"nations which came against Jerusalem shall even go up from year to year to worship the King, the LORD of hosts, and to keep the feast of tabernacles."*

Isaiah 2:2-3 says, *"Come ye, and let us go up to the mountain of the LORD, to the house of the God of Jacob; and he will teach us of his ways, and we will walk in his paths: for out of Zion shall go forth the law, and the word of the LORD from Jerusalem."* These words are confirmed in Micah 4:1-2.

So, we ask "What is the law that will go forth from Jerusalem?" While it will probably not be the Law of Moses, as such, can we really imagine that there be no law of Christ (God) in the Kingdom?

The Law of Moses was a national law that covered all aspects of life. It is hard to assume that the law of God in the Kingdom will only be verbal and rely on man's memory, especially considering it is related to a worldwide Kingdom, lasting a thousand years.

God is a God of order. Would not Christ the King establish His laws to be taught and administered by the Saints, under the righteous rule of Christ and the blessedness of the Kingdom Age? The earth's population is expected to be huge, and for them, such a law seems appropriate. Could the "Sermon on the Mount" be indicative? Could it be the policy speech of the King relating to His future Kingdom?

As far as Bro. Henry Sulley's plan is concerned, in *"A Handbook on The Temple of Ezekiel's Prophecy,"* Bro. Roberts writes,

"All who know Bro. Sulley in his professional capacity, know that it is impossible for a poor job to get out of his hands. His exposition is:

- Based on complete reverence of Divine wording.
- Scrupulously given place to every jot and tittle.
- Hebrew is not "squeezed."
- Size is in harmony with its requirements.

While his interpretation is stated to be highly "idiosyncratic" (meaning peculiar or individual), he was a qualified architect and reference to other architects' opinions must be treated with care. They would either be atheists or "Christians" and would hardly endorse a work that demands the return of Christ to establish God's Kingdom on earth.

The fact is, we have a highly

respected brother who spent months, probably years, on his painstaking work to expound the visions given to Ezekiel. It is reported that he was assisted by Bro. J.W. Thirtle of Hanly, in the translation of the technical expressions in the Hebrew text. Even if his views are disagreed with, on Scriptural grounds, of course, should his efforts not be respected and appreciated? To judge them as just personal opinion and unscriptural, to me, is not wise. The treatise presented by the Apostle Paul in 1 Cor. 8 surely must have a bearing."

The re-introduction of animal sacrifices is challenging, I agree, and matters raised by Bro. Booker is compelling. However, how do we rationalize Jeremiah 33:17-18?

For thus saith the LORD; David shall never want a man to sit upon the throne of the house of Israel; Neither shall the priests the Levites want a man before me to offer burnt offerings, and to kindle meat offerings, and to do sacrifice continually.

Verse 20 confirms this covenant is likened to His covenant of Day and night, which cannot be broken.

Isaiah 56:6-7 confirms that *"The sons of strangers that join themselves to the LORD." "Their sacrifices shall be accepted upon mine altar."*

Psalm 51:18, 19 says, *"Do good in thy good pleasure unto Zion: build thou the walls of Jerusalem. Then shalt thou be pleased with the sacrifices of righteousness, with burnt offering and whole burnt offering: then shall they offer bullocks upon thine altar."*

Isaiah 60:7 says, *"All the flocks of Kedar shall be gathered together unto thee, the rams of Nebaioth shall minister unto thee: they shall come up with acceptance on mine altar, and I will glorify the house of my glory."*

Will these sacrifices serve as a memorial to the mortal population in the Kingdom Age of the atoning work of the Lord Jesus Christ?

Yes, it will be a matter of looking backward, but do we not do so do week by week, when we memorialize the Lord's sacrifice made over 2000 years ago?

Our baptism is, likewise, symbolic of the Lord's sacrifice, as so beautifully described in Romans 6:3-4.

Book 2 on *Psalms*, distributed by the Christadelphian Scripture Study Service, records,

"David appears to reach forward into the Kingdom, when sacrifices and offerings will be restored upon Mt. Zion (Ezek 43:12-27) so that the mortal people can be taught that their "old man" must be put to death like the animals, and their bodies presented as living sacrifices, if they would attain to the glorified state of the immortalized saints. With the risen and glorified Christ then reigning as King over the whole earth, the way of the cross as the way to life might otherwise be obscured. Our need to be crucified with Christ would be lost without vital example of sacrifice to reinforce the essential need to put off the "old man" with its deceitful lusts (Eph 4:22) and show forth Christ's death to sin by the way we live."

Please do not take these comments as a criticism of the article in question but rather to provide a balance in the love of Christ. To me, and I doubt that I am on my own, the Temple outlined by Bro. Sulley is a beacon of hope, and one day we, in God's mercy, may dwell in the house of the LORD forever. I do believe these comments are in keeping with your excellent article under the theme: *"Tear Down or Build."*

Garry Kortman,
Victor Harbor Ecclesia, SA

AUTHOR RESPONSE

First of all, I want to thank Bro. Garry for his letter. I welcome all comments and criticisms.

In his letter Bro. Garry includes quotes from some well-known Christadelphians whom I respect. However, their statements express opinions without proof texts.

I have always respected Bro. John Thomas, partly for his expositions but even more so for his willingness to change his mind when he made a mistake. Some of his "Rules for Bible Study" are listed below:

1. Investigate what you believe.

2. Keep an open mind, and do not be afraid of the results.

3. Do not rely on any human authority for the last word.

In essence, "Do your homework (i.e., Bible study), and don't jump to a conclusion without examining the meanings of key words and the context of the passage under consideration."

I do not doubt Bro. Henry Sulley's professional qualifications as an architect. But a careful study of Ezekiel 40-48 suggests that Bro. Sulley gave more attention to his personal view of a millennial temple than he did to the relevant chapters of the text. Ezekiel describes a much more conventional temple with conventional dimensions—a temple that could have been built in the days of Ezra, Nehemiah, Haggai, Zechariah, and Zerubbabel the prince.

Bro. Sulley did not lay down a Scriptural "foundation" before starting to "build" his own vision of a millennial temple. It appears to me that he had already made up his mind as to the design of his Temple without carefully investigating Ezekiel 40-48. In doing so, he wound up building his interpretation of God's house, not on solid rock but rather on "sand."

According to Ezekiel, this specific temple would be built along the line of Solomon's Temple, where frequent animal sacrifices were normal and expected and necessary—but with no reference at all to Christ and his coming Kingdom.

I leave it to readers to consider the evidence in my previous articles. One cannot reconcile (a) Bro. Sulley's huge Millennial Temple set in the coming Kingdom with (b) the prophet Ezekiel's description of a temple that is served by mortal "priests" who sweat and die, and are presided over by a prince—not the Messiah, but a mortal prince—who marries and has children, one of which will replace him when he dies.

If these two "temples" are the same, then it is also very difficult to understand how Ezekiel fails to mention a coming King/Messiah who will preside over a temple such as Bro. Sulley describes.

At this point, we might ask ourselves a simple but potentially uncomfortable question: Have we become so enthralled with the idea of a huge "Millennial Temple," larger than any other building in human history, that we would cast aside the undeniably more glorious spiritual "temple" of living "stones" being built all around us? I speak of the "temple" in which the Lamb of God, Jesus Christ, would serve as the chief cornerstone (1 Pet 2:6).

I'll rephrase—and this might sting: Which should we revere and worship? Jesus Christ, the perfect once-and-for-all sacrifice for our sins, who has become God's special "temple" (Isa 28:16; 1 Pet 2:6; Eph 2:20-22)—dispensing the *"unsearchable riches"* of love, mercy, grace, peace, and eternal life (Eph 3:8)? Or a towering mass of wood and stone, gold and precious jewels, testifying only to the ingenuity of its architect, but failing to accomplish anything for our salvation?

Isaiah 56:7 is often referenced when considering Bro. Sulley's book: *"My house will be called a house of prayer for all nations."* Many seem to infer from this verse that:

- All nations will be required to visit Jerusalem regularly; and therefore,
- The largest building ever imagined must be erected in Jerusalem to accommodate the vast millions who must travel there.

However, there is a different conclusion: In the Bible, the word "house" (Heb. *bayith* or *beth*, and Greek *oikos*) may mean much more than a simple house. The lexicons tell us that, both in Old and New Testaments, *"house"* may refer to any building (including, of course. a temple), but also to an ordinary house and to a family (because they live in a house), and also to any group of people with common interests, such as a clan or a tribe, or a church or ecclesia. This leads us to a crucial point; any group of believers—whether small or large or even the whole number of believers who are scattered across the earth—can be described as the *"house of God"* (Gen 28:17; Heb 3:2,5; 10:21; 1 Cor 1:16; Eph 2:19; Phil 4:22; 1 Tim 3:15; 2 Tim 1:16).

Returning to Isaiah 56:7 and the idea of "a house of prayer for all nations," the text suggests that:

- In the Kingdom Age, the knowledge and glory of the LORD will cover the earth as the waters cover the sea (Num 14:21; Isa 11:9; Hab 2:14); and
- Wherever believers are, across the vastness of this world, their prayers will unfailingly reach the Lord God and His Son, and receive appropriate answers, for the believers are "the house of God."
- And so, wherever believers are assembled, their prayers will be as efficacious as those of anyone who stands at a "temple" in Jerusalem.

Some might say: "But all believers, and believers-to-be, will need to go up to Jerusalem—in person!—to be instructed and to see sacrifices offered at the Grand Temple in Jerusalem."

The answer to this should be: "Have you heard of radio and television, or the internet and Zoom meetings? Or, have you forgotten that the immortal saints will be able to travel anywhere they please, in a moment or a twinkling of the eye?" We live in an era of human history when we can actually appreciate almost-instantaneous communication worldwide—right now! How much more powerful and transformative will the Kingdom be for mankind compared to what we have now?

I will finish with one more thought: Like many of you, I have often meditated on what the Kingdom of God will be like. For me, what makes such meditation real is thinking about being in the presence of my Lord Jesus Christ—in a more tangible way than is possible now. John's first letter comes to mind: *"That which we have heard, which we have seen with our eyes, and our hands have touched,* [is] *the Word of Life."* (1 John 1:1).

Will we, like John and Christ's other disciples, actually see, hear and touch Jesus then? The prospect of such intimate fellowship makes the Kingdom real to me, real and inexpressibly beautiful—and unbelievably personal when we gaze at the marks and the wounds testifying to what he has done for us all.

I can imagine the ultimate *"marriage supper of the Lamb"* (Rev 19:7-9; Matt 22:2-8; Luke 12:36), a worldwide breaking of bread in the most exalted communion, while everyone celebrates the glorious wonders of God's re-created world.

To me those pictures represent our salvation and the Kingdom of God, which I hope for with all my heart.

But upon all this, let us superimpose Bro. Sulley's ideas: herds of bellowing cattle, bleating sheep, and goats being slaughtered. Their blood stains the ground and the robes of the priests. The fire constantly burns on the altar. The sights and sounds, and smells are overwhelming. Meanwhile, here at the same time, is the Son of God, Jesus Christ. His new robes are spotless, and he himself is the one true and perfect sacrifice.

Will people really need more demonstrations of countless animals being slaughtered, when they can actually see, right before their eyes, the man who—having fulfilled the Law (Matt 5:17)—has made any such further sacrifices meaningless?

Is that what the Kingdom of God will really be like? Maybe it is. Maybe it will be just like that. And if so, then the fault will be mine for not understanding or appreciating it as I should. But something inside me keeps whispering: "This just doesn't seem right." And so I must seek to understand better what I believe.

What do you think?

George Booker, Austin Leander Ecclesia, TX

HISTORY

BETHEL

A CHURCH ASSOCIATED WITH JOHN THOMAS ALMOST 200 YEARS AGO

By Peter Hemingray

STILL standing today is a church which is the last vestige of the time John Thomas spent on a farm in Amelia County, Virginia, about 40 miles southwest of Richmond. As I wrote in late March 2023, it is about to be auctioned and likely soon to be demolished. Thomas lived on the farm from 1837-1839, and close by is this little non-descript church called Bethel in the tiny town of Jetersville. The church was built in 1827 and was still used until around 1973. It was briefly a stronghold of the followers of John Thomas and saw his presence multiple times and also served as the host of a semi-annual meeting of the Brethren in May 1839. The farm of John Thomas is long bereft of any evidence of his presence and is about eight miles from Jetersville, as was his "home" church in Painesville, also long since demolished.

You can find the congregation of Bethel writing in support of John Thomas in his first magazine, the Apostolic Advocate, in 1838. In fact, one of its elders was the agent for this magazine from 1834. Unfortunately, John Thomas left for Illinois in late 1839, and by the time he returned to the area around 1845, his local support no longer included this church, which had returned to the Campbellites. The building later became a Presbyterian church and is currently in poor shape. Even the house on whose land it sits has been vacant for a few years. Soon, only these pictures will remind us of the long-ago era when John Thomas spoke to a welcoming audience.

Peter Hemingray,
Pittsburgh Ecclesia, PA

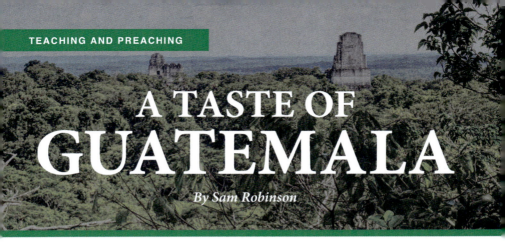

TEACHING AND PREACHING

A TASTE OF GUATEMALA

By Sam Robinson

LAST October, Sis. Martha Osborn and I had the privilege of joining my parents on their yearly trip to Guatemala. It was our first time traveling outside North America, so we were very excited but unsure of what to expect since neither of us knew how to speak Spanish! We arrived early in the afternoon on Thursday and were greeted at the airport by Israel, who is currently studying for baptism. He took us to his home, where we met his wife, Sis. Victoria, and spent the afternoon talking and touring around the city. The next morning our hosts had thoughtfully made and delivered breakfast to our hotel room—*chuchitos*, small Guatemalan tamales. Though entirely different from our North American version of breakfast, it was quite good! We spent the next hour or so exploring the city and then hopped on a bus with some other brothers, sisters, family, and friends and made the hour-long drive to Antigua. There we explored the old buildings and streets, Guatemalan shops, beautiful scenery, and enjoyed a "typical" Guatemalan lunch. We were already starting to love the food, mostly because of the fresh tortillas provided with anything and everything you might eat. Our bus driver even spent the day touring with us, and Bro. Encarnación seemed to have a very interesting conversation with him about the Truth over lunch.

Bro. Eduardo Mate with the group in Guatemala

On Saturday, we had scheduled two Bible classes in the afternoon. My dad led the classes as we sat in a circle in the courtyard of Israel and Victoria's home. One was on King Manasseh, and the other on the Memorial emblems. There were just over ten of us there. As it got dark, we had to devise some interesting ways to light the space. For someone used to the typical buildings and setups we have in Canada, this way of meeting in the open air somehow felt more genuine. Martha and I were sadly unable to understand the classes, though we did try using Google Translate's real-time translation. It mostly led to us trying not to laugh at the poor translation. Instead, we spent the time reading or working on our own studies. After the classes, as Martha and I were sitting around wondering what to do (it's amazing how lacking communication can weigh on you after a few days), the son of Bro. Jaime and Sis. Karla introduced himself. He was about our age, and we could have some basic conversation using Google Translate, which was really exciting! After the classes, we went out as a group to dinner, where we were able to fit in a bit better with everyone there. One sister's husband joined us for dinner and could speak fluent English. He made sure to sit by us and help us have further conversations with the others there.

Sunday was our last full day. We ate at Pollo Campero for breakfast for the third day in a row, and attended Sunday School and the Memorial service (Bro. Jaime, who was visiting from El Salvador, gave the exhortation).

We then went out with the group to Pollo Campero (again) for lunch. We returned to the home of Israel and Sis. Victoria, and spent the afternoon talking (or trying to). We then spent an hour singing hymns. It's a very special memory looking back at the small group united in something so important, despite incredibly different backgrounds. The next morning a sister offered to drive us to the airport, and we were on our way home again. It was an incredible experience, seeing a different culture, meeting new brothers and sisters, and seeing how they live. As I'm sure many trips like this show, it was amazing to see how the Truth can bring together people with very different backgrounds.

Sam Robinson,
Brant County Ecclesia, ON

Bro. Sam Robinson and Sis. Martha Osborn

TEACHING AND PREACHING

A NEW PREACHING RESOURCE

By Art Courtenel

GOD continues to bless the extended preaching work of www.christadelphianvideo.org, and we are thrilled to announce that we are now at the primary stages of the next development of the christadelphianvideo.org network of sites. This includes the development of the revamped worldwide preaching arm of the network (formally known as *Bible Truth and Prophecy*) and now known as **Discover the Bible**.

We have firmly established christadelphianvideo.org as the largest collection for peer-reviewed, globally sourced and produced central video material for the community. Thousands of brothers and sisters worldwide use these videos daily. This next project will become our outreach arm and will be focused entirely on the viewing public.

Building on our experience with christadelphianvideo.org we will be developing from the ground up new graphics, navigation and functionality, an app, and hopefully brand-new bespoke preaching videos of differing lengths. These will cover a broad spectrum of Bible subjects, seminars, live events, and linked social media accounts, as well as possibly utilizing some preaching material from christadelphianvideo. org. We are also developing a new-look graphics package, a direction plan, a site map, and collaborations with other Christadelphian sites (e.g., thisisyourbible.com) to utilize their correspondence functionality.

Please let us know by email if this is something you would be interested in being involved in: providing video material (either Individually or ecclesially), volunteering time or ideas or learning more about how you can contribute. No experience is needed; at first, we will be engaged in dialogue to determine the basics highlighted above. Once we have a plan of action, we will move to the next stage of creating the site with our webmaster, and we will need assistance with that also. Please contact us at christadelphianvideo@gmail.com. There are God-given opportunities for everyone to witness for the Truth we love and cherish. This is just another one of those opportunities!

May God continue to bless all our efforts in his service according to his will.

Art Courtenel,
Rugby Ecclesia, UK

Thoughts on the Way

Why are There Two Different Emblems?

WHY are there two different emblems—bread and wine—at the memorial meeting?

The obvious answer is that the bread represents Christ's body, and the wine represents his blood. But that answer seems inadequate since either one alone could symbolize Christ's sacrificial death. Is there some further reason?

The bread represents the strength of Christ's **life**, a life totally dedicated to the will of the Father. The wine particularly represents his **death**; the blood willingly poured out as a climax to his life's work. And the wine could also suggest the joy of all believers' reunion with Jesus Christ:

> I will not drink of this fruit of the vine from now on until that day when I drink it anew with you in my Father's kingdom. (Matt 26:29).

In the upper room, the bread was broken and passed to each disciple. Then each disciple drank a portion of the wine. But this does not mean that Christ can be divided or that we believers should be broken or divided from one another. **All the blessings belong to every individual among us!** The body which the bread represents, that is, Christ's spiritual "body" of believers, cannot be broken. It is one:

> Because there is one loaf, we, who are many, are one body. (1 Cor 10:17).

Paul goes on to say that the body is united, *"held together"* or *"supported"* (*"knit together"* KJV), in love with the Head, who is Christ himself (Col 2:2,19). As the natural body is held together by ligaments and sinews and nurtured together through a single circulatory system, the spiritual body is bound together by love, especially Christ's love.

A Funeral

Our memorial service is like a funeral in *"proclaiming the Lord's death until he comes."* (1 Cor 11:26). In attending a funeral, we show respect for the deceased and for the occasion. We also recognize, for ourselves as well, the solemnity of both life and death and how, in our daily lives, we come in contact with eternal things. "Ask not for whom the bell tolls; it tolls for thee." Surely, if we grasp this fact, we need not worry that we will forget to examine ourselves.

A Funeral and a Celebration

Of course, this is a unique funeral because the one who was dead is now alive, gloriously and eternally alive. The joy of this fact will offset the seriousness of the occasion: The one who died for each of us is alive forevermore. What a promise there is in our Lord's words:

> Hallelujah! For our Lord God Almighty reigns. Let us rejoice and be glad and give him glory! For the wedding of the Lamb has come, and his bride has made herself ready. (Rev 19:6,7).

Every memorial meeting helps us to remember and reaffirm to ourselves the basis of our faith:

- that Christ is our Head;
- that he died for each of us;
- that we all belong to him;
- and consequently, we also belong to one another;
- that we are all honor-bound to love one another, and
- care for one another no matter how difficult that may seem to be;
- that we must forgive one another even as we are forgiven by God;
- that this life is not an end in itself but a preparation for the age to come;
- and that our Savior, Jesus Christ, is coming again.

If this is our spirit and attitude on such occasions, we will show Christ's death, resurrection, and love until he comes.

At the memorial table, we see a funeral and we also see a king coming in royal glory. We must put these two ideas together and hold both of them in our minds at the same time. When we prepare or serve the emblems or partake of them, we are thinking of the terrible death of a perfect man. But concurrently, we can rejoice because we know a new creation is dawning in his resurrection and his promise: *"I will come again."* (John 14:3).

*George Booker,
Austin Leander Ecclesia, TX*

THE CHRISTADELPHIAN
TIDINGS
OF THE KINGDOM OF GOD

is published monthly, except bimonthly in July-August, by The **Christadelphian Tidings**, 567 Astorian Drive, Simi Valley, CA 93065-5941. **FIRST CLASS POSTAGE PAID** at Simi Valley, CA and at additional mailing offices. POSTMASTER: Send address changes to The Christadelphian Tidings, 567 Astorian Dr., Simi Valley, CA 93065.

Christadelphian Tidings Publishing Committee: Alan Markwith (Chairman), Joe Hill, John Bilello, Peter Bilello, Linda Beckerson, Nancy Brinkerhoff, Shawn Moynihan, Kevin Flatley, Jeff Gelineau, William Link, and Ken Sommerville.

Christadelphian Tidings Editorial Committee: Dave Jennings (Editor), Section Editors: Nathan Badger (Life Application), TBA (Exhortation and Consolation), Jessica Gelineau (Music and Praise), Steve Cheetham (Exposition), Richard Morgan (First Principles), Dave Jennings (Teaching and Preaching), Jan Berneau (CBMA/C), George Booker, (Thoughts on the Way, Q&A), John Bilello (Letters to the Editor), Jeff Gelineau (News and Notices, Subscriptions), Melinda Flatley (Writer Recruitment and Final Copy), and Shawn Moynihan (Books).

Subscriptions: The Tidings Magazine is provided **FREE** for any who would like to read it. The Magazine is available in PDF Format online at **tidings.org**. If you would like to order a printed subscription to **The Tidings** you may do so simply by making a donation to cover the printing costs. The Suggested Donation for printing and shipping is **USD $70.00;** (we ask for a Minimum Donation of USD $35.00 for a printed subscription.)

All subscription information is available online at **www.tidings.org**. You may subscribe online and make donations online or by mail to the above address. Information on how to subscribe in other countires is also available online at **www.tidings.org/subscribe**.

The Christadelphian Tidings is published on the 15th of the month for the month following. Items for publication must be received by the 1st of the month. Correspondence to the editor, Dave Jennings at **editor@tidings.org**. Publication of articles does not presume editorial endorsement except on matters of fundamental doctrine as set forth in the BASF. Letters should be sent via e-mail to **letters@tidings.org**. Please include your name, address and phone number. The magazine reserves the right to edit all submissions for length and clarity.

©2023, Tidings Publishing Committee. In the spirit of Christ ask for permission before reproducing any material. Contact us at **editor@tidings.org**

Made in the USA
Middletown, DE
13 April 2023

28696062R00038